The Sophist

CHARLES BERNSTEIN was born in Manhattan in 1950. He has published 27 collections of poetry including *With Strings* (University of Chicago Press, 2001), *Republics of Reality: Poems 1975–1984* (Sun & Moon, 2000) and *Controlling Interests* (reprinted by Roof in 2004). His essays are included in *My Way: Speeches and Poems* (Chicago, 1999) and *Content's Dream: Essays 1975–1984* (reprinted by Northwestern University Press, 2001). Bernstein is a professor at the University of Pennsylvania. Author page: epc.buffalo.edu.

The Sophist

CHARLES BERNSTEIN

Introduction by Ron Silliman

S
SALT

CAMBRIDGE

PUBLISHED BY SALT PUBLISHING
PO Box 937, Great Wilbraham, Cambridge PDO CB1 5JX United Kingdom
PO Box 202, Applecross, Western Australia 6153

First published by Sun & Moon Press 1987
Second edition 2004

Printed and bound in the United Kingdom by Lightning Source

Typeset in Swift 9.5 / 13

ISBN 1 84471 000 9 paperback

SP

1 3 5 7 9 8 6 4 2

Contents

The Text, the Beloved?
Bernstein's *Sophist*
By Ron Silliman

In 1987, when Sun & Moon Press first published *The Sophist*, Charles Bernstein was already one of the dozen or so best known poets of his generation, having gained an enormous amount of visibility as co-editor of the magazine *L=A=N=G=U=A=G=E* (1978–81). In the eleven years since he first self-published *Parsing* under the Erving Goffmanesque imprint of Asylum's Press, Bernstein had published ten additional books of poetry, a collection of essays, *Content's Dream*, co-edited his journal, plus an anthology based on it published by Southern Illinois University Press, as well as features on language poetry & environs in both the *Paris Review* & *boundary 2*.

In retrospect, it's almost hard to remember the primitive nature of some of those earliest publications—not only was *Parsing* basically photocopied and stapled, its cover the dark blue stock you would get for a report cover at Kinko's, but *Shade*, Bernstein's first "large" collection from Sun & Moon was stapled & Xeroxed as well, the first volume in that press' Contemporary Literature series, an edition of just 500. With the exception of the S.I.U.P collection from *L=A=N=G=U=A=G=E*, Bernstein's publications up to 1987 had all the features of any poet in the small presses. Some came from presses that disappeared quickly, such as Pod Books or Awede. One, *Islets / Irritations*, was initially published by Jordan Davies, who, in lieu of having a more formal imprint, simply listed his name as publisher. Others were either slender suites suitable for chapbooks, such as *Stigma*, or, in the case of both *Legend* (co-authored with Bruce Andrews, Ray Di Palma, Steve McCaffery & yours truly) and *The Occurrence of Tune*, contained just one poem.

Regardless of how or where they were printed, Bernstein's first three large collections, *Shade* (1978), *Controlling Interests* (1980), and *Islets / Irritations* (1983), were impeccable instances of the well-constructed book of poems. Indeed, after the publication of *Controlling Interests* by Roof Books, Bernstein's reputation as a major American poet has never been in question.

An unwritten premise of the well-formed book of poems has to do with the self-similarity of its contents. The poems tend—that verb's flexibility is important—to look alike. They're approximately the same size, the line lengths and stanzaic strategies similar from poem to poem. If the poems are all relatively short, there may be one or two longer ones, or a suite of linked shorter pieces, that constitute the organizing works around which the book is built.

In the 1950s and '60s, the form was so set that the Wesleyan poets of that generation in particular appeared to have come all from the same cookie-cutter, regardless of any differences otherwise between poets: the "major" work could be a poem between six and 15 pages long, surrounded by shorter pieces that tended to be one or two pages each. That's a form that John Ashbery would caricature mercilessly in his "award-winning" pseudo-academic period of the 1970s & into the '80s.

By the 1980s the form has loosened up a little, but only just. There are more books with "longer" poems—five or six pages apiece—but self-similarity is still the organizing principle underlying the construction of most books. Louis Zukofsky, whose longpoem *"A"* represents the most thorough meditation on part:whole relations within the poem, touches on this aspect ever so lightly with *"A"*-16, a four-word text set alongside others that go up as high as *"A"*-12's 135 pages. But it appears that it never occurred to Zukofsky to stick a section of *"A"* in amongst the poems that will eventually be compiled into *Complete Short Poetry* when they appeared in individual collections. Similarly, Olson never thought to mix *Maximus* & non-Max poems into a single volume, tho generally only the most devoted Olson acolyte could tell what constituted a Max & what did not. The volumes of Robert Creeley, Frank O'Hara, Jack Spicer, whomever, all follow these same unwritten rules.

As do virtually all of the early volumes on the language poets.

Consider, for example, alternative genres. CDs (or, earlier, tapes & records) from music, or gallery exhibitions of visual artists. A painter may work in different modes, but generally a given exhibit is going to focus on just one, or possibly two that are very closely related. Mickey Hart is not about to bring his anthropological explorations of drumming to his recordings with the Grateful Dead. Brian Eno & Gabriel Byrne put their sound collage pieces onto a single album, *My Life in the Bush of Ghosts*, rather than their own records. Part of what made Harry Partch, the hobo composer who worked not only with invented instruments but his own 72-tone scale, seem like such a nutjob was that some of his self-issued recordings included not just his works, but dry, even tedious lectures about his theories of music.

The Sophist is a jumble, a jungle, a jangle of—dare I say?—overdetermined elements hodged-podged together. If it has an antecedent—there are in fact a few—perhaps the most direct is the conservatory at Citizen Kane's Xanadu, an interior shot for which the ever-resourceful director Orson Welles (a man with more than a little of the Bernstein in him, or verse visa) matted in footage from an old RKO pre-historic adventure. Thus in the background of this too-lush garden one sees a pterodactyl in flight. Work after work in this book proceeds likewise, the obvious & the impossible in a constant, slightly frenetic mambo, not by virtue of reinforcing & building upon the unwritten law of self-sameness, as books of poems *are supposed to* but rather just its opposite—as if each text were antithetical, pushing as hard as could be to establish a new space not announced or even fathomable from what's come before.

Bernstein himself says as much at the outset of the opening poem, coyly titled "The Simply":

Nothing can contain the empty stare that ricochets
haphazardly against any purpose. My hands
are cold but I see nonetheless with an infrared
charm.

Sentence after sentence in "The Simply" skates always in different directions—*ricochets* is very literal here, as is the claim that *Nothing can contain* this—until, seven pages downstream, one arrives at an equally straightforward denouement:

> "You have such a horrible sense of equity which
> is inequitable because there's no such
> thing as equity." *The text, the beloved?*
> Can I stop living when the pain gets too
> great? Nothing interrupts this moment.
> False.

As is always the case in Bernstein's work, that which appears as if written "haphazardly" is in fact obsessively scripted—*equity* in that first sentence in all of its conceivable meanings, including in that last instance real estate. Similarly *Nothing interrupts* is not the denial of action, but rather the naming of its actor. It's a dizzying performance, intended I think to connect the reader with the Bernstein of his earlier books, familiar in his lushness, dazzling in the constant display of jaw-dropping devices, drenching us in the humidity of these tropes.

It took me more than one reading of *The Sophist* to understand why, at the conclusion of "The Simply," Bernstein takes a step back rather than going forward. I think it is to lure readers in, particularly those who have not yet sipped from the langpo Kool-Aid. On the surface, at least, "The Voyage of Life" is a simpler, more traditional poem than "The Simply," whereas the works that immediately follow thereafter:

- A dense prose piece bordering on a story entitled "Fear and Trespass"
- The daft one-act play entitled "Entitlement" (it might have been called "Seven Scenes in Seven Pages") whose characters consist of Liubov Popova, Jenny Lind, and John Milton
- A poem titled "Outrigger," whose text comes across as carefully bonkers, its lineation—its key relationship to the

principle of self-sameness—extra leaded, literally, lines spaced more or less at "one-and-one-half spaces"

- "The Years as Swatches," a long single stanza composed of very short lines—only one line runs four words long, only six run three
- Another story, "The Only Utopia Is in a Now (Another Side of Gagenga . . . frent)
- A 16-line two-stanza poem entitled, "From Lines of Swinburne"
- Another poem, "Special Pleading," that opens up its lineation
- A poem entirely composed of short bits divided by asterisks in the manner of Ted Berrigan
- "Dysraphism," one of Bernstein's signature poems, roughly in the manner of "The Simply," whose title Bernstein explains in a rather chatty footnote
- "By Cuff," a poem of just five lines
      Flew, then flew
      through the hall
      then flew
      a wasted monument
      recalled to perfidy
- "Hitch World," a three-page poem of dense, but not necessarily deep, stanzas
- "Like DeCLAraTionS in a HymIE CEMetArY," which begins
      WheTHer oriented or RETurned tO
      sTAndiNg poSTurE
      ACCUMULAteD
      advicement and bASicALly

Try sneaking that one through spell-check. The purpose of this list, which characterizes the first 50 of over 170 pages, is to give a sense of how like a gyroscope *The Sophist* proceeds, perpetually off-balance, lunging, lurching from text to text, its only "center" something that each of this works conceivably points to but which proves impossible to nail. It is somewhere in between all of the above.

Seventeen years later, after books like Charles Bernstein's *A Poetics* and *My Way*, *The Sophist* doesn't necessarily look as radical to the eye as perhaps it once did. Significantly, both of those texts are more apt to be characterized as critical—collections of essays into which poetry "intrudes." Bernstein's own books of poems, such as *With Strings*, have in fact moved back to something closer to what we might expect from a "normal book." At least the selfsame principle appears more visible there. That something that has taken deeper root in Bernstein's "professional" writing than in his "creative" work should have shown up first here in *The Sophist* is itself worth thinking about.

As are precedents. The two I think are most visible are William Carlos Williams' *Spring & All*, a volume that appeared nearly 50 years before anybody was ready to "get it" back in 1923, mixing Williams' most deeply condensed poems into the hot broth of the most radical poetics text that had, at that late modern moment, been written. Williams' book sunk more or less without a trace, odd enough under any circumstance but positively bizarre given just how famous some of its poems—"The Red Wheel Barrow," "The Pure Products of America"—later became, tho largely due to being read in WCW's various collected editions. It wasn't until Harvey Brown produced what may have been a pirate edition of the original volume in 1970 that a much later generation of poets found themselves dumbstruck at the brilliance of Williams' total project. I would argue that the organization of *The Sophist* follows *Spring & All* not in its "linked verse in a critical frame," but rather because the construction of the book itself is understood by its author as a critical act. Which is why it follows that this principle follows Bernstein into his prose more than into his later poetry.

The second source is one that Bernstein sort of half gives away in a title's allusion amidst the poems I listed—Robert Duncan, particularly the Duncan of *Roots and Branches* & *Bending the Bow*. In many respects, The Sophist is very nearly a direct descendant of Duncan's project, mixing as the San Francisco writer's did prose, plays, individual poems, translations, as well as—contra Zukofsky, contra Olson—sections of his ongoing long works, *Passages* and *The Structure of Rime*.

But whereas Duncan understood his commingling of divergent texts as part of a larger organic relation that could be traced back to his life (with some fudging as to chronology in the process, especially in the first of his trio of books, *The Opening of the Field*), the New Yorker Bernstein doesn't buy into the mystical self-justifications—a defensive wall more than anything else—that Duncan erected around his work. Bernstein's text in this sense forms an argument, not an autobiography. It is worth noting that in the opening of "Outrigger," the piece that immediately precedes "The Years as Swatches," Bernstein adapts a device taken directly from Duncan's "The Fire, *Passages 13*," a little grid of phrases apparently with no connection one to the other that nonetheless build tonally.* "The Years as Swatches" appears more Zukofskian with its hyper-narrow lines than the echo of Duncan's *The Years as Catches* might suggest, but its concerns with speech & the ontological status of language directly address this question:

Voice seems
to break
over these
short lines
cracking or
setting loose.
I see a word
& it repeats
itself as
your location
overt becalm
that neither
binds nor furnishes:
articles of
cancelled
port

* Bernstein will return to it again later in the ninth section of "A Person is Not an Entity Symbolic but the Divine Incarnate."

in which I
see you
&
changed by the
mood
return to
sight of
our encounter.
My heart
cleaves
in twos
always
to this
promise
that we
had known but
have forgotten
along the way.
Maze of chaliced
gleam a
menace in
the eyes
clearing
once again.
Gravity's loss:
weight of
hazard's probity
remaindered
on the lawn's
intransigent
green.
Funds deplete
the deeper
fund within
us lode no

one has
found.
And yet
as if, when all –
should current
flood its
days
& self
renounce
in concomitant
polity.

This is one of those moments, and poems, in which one might say
Bernstein is being startlingly literal. *He means this.* The argument here
between politics (the market) and the self ("the deeper / fund within")
comes down clearly in favor of the Enlightenment, even if it is an
Enlightenment thoroughly conditioned with a hard-earned cynicism.
It is precisely this commitment that will enable the most comic poet
of his generation to be, in the same moment, one of the most political.

The Sophist in this sense is a hinge text, for Charles Bernstein & for
poetry.

The Simply

Nothing can contain the empty stare that ricochets

haphazardly against any purpose. My hands

are cold but I see nonetheless with an infrared

charm. Beyond these calms is a coast, handy but

worse for abuse. Frankly, hiding an adumbration of collectible

cathexis, catheterized weekly, burred and bumptious;

actually, continually new groups being brought forward for

drowning. We get back, I forget to call, we're

very tired eating. They think they'll get salvation, but

this is fraudulent. Proud as punches—something like

Innsbruck, saddles, sashed case; fret which is whirled

out of some sort of information; since you ask. We're

very, simply to say, smoked by fear, guided by

irritation. Rows of desks. *Something like* after

a while I'm reading my book, go to store to get

more stuff. "You're about as patient as the flame

on a match." After the ceremony lunch was served

by Mrs. Anne MacIssac, Mrs. Betty MacDonald, and Mrs. Catherine

Macleod, and consisted of tea, bannock, homemade cheese

oatcakes and molasses cookies. We thank the ladies. Waste

not, want not; but there's such a thing as being shabby.

Which seems finally to move the matter, but in despair

seeing "lived experience" as only possible under the

hegemony of an ideology, an "imaginary". Started
to do this, I corrected, he (they) demurred, I
moved aside. Don't look up but she goes off. "Pleasant Bay news
really hasn't dropped out, it was just on holiday." To
bare it, make it palpable—but not so it can be
transcended, rather circulated, exposed to air, plowed, worked
until fertile for inhabitation. All huff & puff. Is
having a party and wants us to. House burned, possessions
destroyed, death. Wind howling in the background, Neil drives
over to say there's an urgent message. Get into it, move
through it. These vague reproaches—a handkerchief
waved at the tumultuous facade, returning the look
with an altogether different effect of discounting. Over
and over plagued by the dialectic of such Messianism—tied
as it is to a conviction in a primeval totality of
word and object, each echoing the truth of the other and
the very contours of the cosmic. County Clerk Connie
Murray told council that packing dogs had "pretty much
wiped out MacPhee". But why this paralysis of terror and
extreme guilt feelings that he had to go out of his
way to help us? "For he was working it
for all it was worth, just as it was, no doubt, working
him, and just as the working and the worked were, as

one might explain, the parties to every relation: the

worker in one connection the worked in another." We're

in Sydney, Nova Scotia, maybe hospital cafeteria. Tendenciously

insipient, flaccidly ebullient: transmorgrified pullulation.

Woman says she's very busy but will try to look into

it when its turn comes up. The landscape has

so much the power to overwhelm; walking back

some yards in the yard, up a small hill, the vista

extends to the ocean; the sky is immense, total; the rolling

hills rock into a reverie of place that is sometimes

just distracting, at others like some dream of the pastoral as

living presence. Took elevator to 3, then walked to 4. The

sin of pride, positivity. "I don't think they make people like

him anymore—tough as a boiled owl." On July 31

Fred Timmons, Bayne and Hattie Smith, Mary Sutherland,
   Margaret

Hartford and Lizzie Daniels enjoyed a treat of strawberries

and cream at the home of Grace Kendziora. I am particularly

susceptible to the stuff about angels: do you really think

so? Intrusion of event blasting through to, exaggerated

by, standing in so much more than. 464 moved

to side entrance of 101. This would be the 'now time'

of the communicative moment, reducing as it does to an
   idealization

of nonhistorical, nonspatial—which is to say—antimaterialist
possibility. At some point, later, she meets with an other
official. Though my dreams fail me, surely you will not. Nothing
brought him so sharply, so roundly, to a sense of his
condition as this and no sooner had he outlined the limits
he could, he would, reproach himself for; it was
in a manner of agreement with this new perception that
he was determined to venture onto the scene, equipped, as he
would have it to himself, with the sturdiness of conviction,
however recent, to match with any presented persuasion; it
would not "do" that he had simply donned
his views, as one simply "takes up" the morning papers,
his assessment took well in hand the need to add
recalcitrance to the equipage of his stand; and so
it was with sanguine resignation that he departed. The
bugs practically get the better of you. "For all that
we have not up to the present noticed any more
Religion among these poor savages than among *brutes*;
this is what wrings our hearts with compassion, if
they could know themselves what they themselves are
worth, and what they cost him *who has loved us all*
so much. Now what consoles us in the midst
of this ignorance and barbarism, and what makes us hope

[4]

to see the Faith widely implanted, is partly the *docility*
they have shown in wishing to be instructed, and partly
the honesty and decency we observe in them: for
they listen to us so diligently concerning the mysteries
of our Faith, and repeat after us, *whether they understand
it or not*, all that we declare to them." In the current
debate, idealism is greatly endangered by the common
claim among "Marxists" that indeed *it*, as the cultural
the social is the material base; surely
the task must be to salvage idealism from such
ravages. Why not, under a sway so profoundly
gentle as this, give the act a credence that, in
other light, seemed to demand disapprobriation, the
account of which, at odd measures, might even be
taken if the alarm first not sounds that, painstakingly
no more the proviso than encampment, only to force full
well the recondite consideration that what is by such
confrontation supposed to later allow is just
what by deference, accomodation to vitiate, would
be then available? Adventure film with poison arrows,
seated in front. By objectifying, that is to say
neutralizing one's regard, allowing the integrity
of the other and all that it cedes by its

dominion. The world deals with negation and
contradiction and does not assert any single
scheme. New signs on the federal building, they say
FEDERAL BUILDING. Or whether you're dreaming or just
thinking to yourself. The isolation, the boredom; the
quiet, the space. Why am I not a soul at rest, at
peace? Already around the corner _____ are _____. *But*
it's not pain *but* the fear of pain that is terrifying.
And what price to be so peaceful that nothing
is felt or noticed or perturbs. ANXIETY
IS MORTALITY. Is everything, then, prey to your cannibalizing
search for material? Such visibility suggests radar
patterns, launching pads. "Sketchily clustered even, these
elements gave out that vague pictorial glow which forms
the first appeal of a living 'subject' to the painter's
consciousness, but the glimmer became intense as I
proceeded to further analysis." *They call me* **Mister**
Tibbs. It is the taint of positive value itself in the mythological
structure; to question, that is, all current correspondences
even the most luminous, lusterous. **False**. Today turns
so that I'm trying, only which helps to explain, now
ensconced, as any place has so much fully to; in
any case we're makes more count as to

getting, still it will be good to see what's waiting.

She shirks complexion, resents having had. Vague

feel of it but no recollection. *Ex dulcit figitur omnibus*

plectum semperis delecto, obit relentere moribus dixum.

For I have wintered in the fields of the Hesperus and tasted

of the starling; this, too, unbears my trial. Though

the question is, how can you lose something you never had?

Accumulation of accomodation, inherent entertainment an

muddled portion. *That grown we weep for want of.*

SLUMPS AS IT PUMPS. "I've got my instinct trained

to a rare morsel of respect." That is, that I can see myself.

They produced thick tomato sandwiches, saying with pride

that they were brought from Woolworth's. One screw

missing, but you can air condition us all; some kind of far

away village, behind it. Don't you find it chilly

sitting with your Silly? Yet things

beguile us with their beauty

their sullen irascibility: the hay of the

imagination is the solace of a dry soul; which

is to say, keep yourselves handy since

you may be called on at any hour.

One wants almost to shudder (yawn, laugh . . .) in disbelief

at the hierarchization of consciousness in such a dictum

as "first thought, best thought", as if recovery

were to be prohibited from the kingdom;

for anyway "first thought" is no thinking

at all. There is no 'actual space of'. So

quiet you can hear the clouds gather. Weep

not, want not; but there's such a thing as being

numb. "As if you could kill time without injuring eternity."

I'm screaming at somebody or being screamed at, not

interesting enough to wake up for. Slurps

as it burps. FIRST BURP, BEST BURP. "You take it very well,"

he says admiringly. "I don't think I would have been as

cheerful if Uncle Bill hadn't given me money." The

Case of the Missing Coagulate. *Emphysema* | Nice to see ya.

'Some such succor' 'monozite don't treat

me right' 'infestation of prognostication'.

"You have such a horrible sense of equity which

is inequitable because there's no such

things as equity." *The text, the beloved?*

Can I stop living when the pain gets too

great? Nothing interrupts this moment.

False.

The Voyage of Life

Over the remote hills, which seem
to intercept the stream, and turn
in from its hitherto direct
course, a path is dimly seen, tending
directly toward that cloudy Fabric
which is the object and desire
of the Voyager.
–THOMAS COLE

Resistance marries faith, not faith persist-
Ence. Which is to say, little to import
Or little brewed from told and anxious
Ground: an alternating round of this or
That, some outline that strikes the looking back,
That gives the Punch and Judy to our show.
If it be temperate, it is temper-
Ance that make us hard; by strength of purpose
Turn Pinocchio into ox or gore
Melons with pickaxes, which the fighting
Back in turn proposes slugged advantage,
Slumped discomfit: rashes of ash, as
On a scape to ripple industry with
Hurls, the helter finds in shrubbing stuns. We
Carve and so are carved in twofold swiftness
Of manifold: the simple act of speak-
Ing, having heard, of crossing, having creased.
Sow not, lest reap, and choke on blooming things:
Innovation is Satan's toy, a train
That rails to semblance, place of memory's
Loss. Or tossed in tune, emboss with gloss in-
Signias of air.

Fear and Trespass

I have no deep respect for words—they're my business, after all.
—ROSS MACDONALD

"Give me your cold seas, I will warm them in mine."
—GIORGIO DE CHIRICO

The physical inadequacy of his kiss didn't really matter. He had come from a great distance in the night, through the stormy surf and silent fields, driven only by a vague but persistent pull toward that balcony overhanging the vacant and astonished garden where memory or the memory of memory called like an Alsatian train ascending from the plateau to the mist above the treetops. Under the palm trees and midnight sun, she thought of her father—an apparition from what could have been a primeval era, filled with shadows, abrupt noises, and looming disembodied faces—and had to admit that she hated him; and yet the word hate agitated her and her uneasyness splashed into the sultry evening, reminding her of Tampa summers eating clams by the shore and the children shouting indecipherable expletives at their mothers as they gurgled down their pop and hot dogs. There was not, for either of them, any hope that they would get back what they had lost, fitful as that had been, under the depthless expanse of the starless night, so that the distance that separated them, measured in feet or years, was a gaping void neither dared fling themself into and yet both hoped—a hope as stippled with dissuasion as desire—to be hurled into it despite themselves, their reticences and singular dismay. There would be no further news—the hideous secret that rended their emotions when it resurfaced, as momentarily as a glimmer in the eye of a police sergeant, only to plunge deep into the subterranean forest of remorse and willed blindness—no witless explanations and bathetic excuses, only the tortured insolvency of the moment breaking like a single wave against a sea castle, habitude of the lost or lingering souls of Atlantis, dream-precursors of the Maya, and of their Olmec destiny.

The summer would end, as seasons always did, the shopkeepers boarding up their windows and salting their pork for the larder, the reproachful church masters preparing for the last sermon and the stiffer breeze that would blow away the time, or cast it like a fisherman's rod or cadet's brimmed hat; the summer would end, but not as soon as the night.

Where was this place in which they wrapped their eyes—two trains rattling through a long-deserted tunnel at the end of a prairie—in which their hope was buried miles under the sodden earth and encrusted boulders? Who were these people, recklessly engaged in a reconciliation neither could possibly understand or sustain, drawn together as if by a flame on a matchbook match that was already flickering when ignited, ignoble bannisters on the stairway to eternity's pale encroachment, mutilated by the passage yet hypnotized by the terrain? They could no more turn back than they could push on, puppeted by distractions too indistinct to visualize and too intoxicating to shake loose, nor would such a course impose itself on either of them, dumbfounded as they were by the mention of ideas or places or hearts. They stood on the balcony, mute witnesses to a reality beyond their, dwarfing their, aspirations and compromised despair at the same time as exposing them to the brute alchemy of a dependence to which they knew neither the address nor the cure.

If at the point of death the soul has a power to reach into itself and restore a psychic balance previously held in check for that moment, ready cash for the inevitable reckoning of life's grosses and nets, then such a power could also be tapped at penultimate moments when if not life's end then life's means were in sway—or it was with such an intuition that she drew into herself a deep and troubled breath. She inspected her thoughts like a fussy shopper holding up the seconds toward a fluorescent light thirty feet above the selling floor, pulling at the seams and poking the button holes, picking up new pieces as fast as, and as brusquely as, discarding the old ones, until, amidst what was perhaps a blue-plaid conjecture with too big a collar, he spoke her name, at first so softly that he might have been eating it as he rolled it in his mouth, and then, quite gradually, louder and more plainly. The sound of his voice broke her reverie and she shook her head to clear what gray matter still floated behind her eyes before looking in his direction without, however, looking at him, an irritating habit she had picked up in order to avoid being bothered by strangers but one which, try as she might, informed all her encounters whether with coworkers or local merchants or now with him. Still, the sound, or really sounds, of his voice jolted her and she squinted her eyes in a strained and transparent effort to find his face, which was hard to distinguish from the air or the sound of the radio from the neighbor's patio on which she had grown accustomed to depend for news and relaxation during the long days with no one around except the tradespeople to whom she would sometimes turn for conversation as well as provision. Though convinced of the futility of the visit, it did not occur to him to regret that he had come, or to begin to resent it; sentiment was for people who could afford it, like country clubs and champagne and lobster suppers by a lake, not for someone whose repertory of feelings began at recalcitrance and ended with indifference, who was as oblivious to the unexpressed pain of others as he was to his own chasm of unrequited desperation and chained venality. Neither did he choose to indulge in desultory speculation about the failings of his childhood, if only his mother had soothed him more and reprimanded less he might not have had to do what he had to do, the thought of his mother, of whom he had no conscious memory, sending cold chills into his stomach and down his legs until his knees buckled with the force of his introspection and the increasingly frigid night air. He left as he had come, unknown to the place where he arrived and ungiving to it, a hawk descending for a view of a prey projected by a hunger he does not recognize and so never ceases to indulge, gracefully and indigently.

Entitlement

Cast:

Liubov Popova (1889–1924): Russian constructivist/futurist painter, who abandoned easel paintings in 1921 in favor of a productivist concern for industrial and theatrical design. She died of scarlet fever contracted from her child.

Jenny Lind (1820–87): Swedish coloratura soprano. Under the management of P.T. Barnum she toured the U.S. as the "Swedish Nightingale" (1850–52).

John Milton (1608–74): Puritan revolutionary and radical anti-monarchist, served as propagandist and minister in Oliver Cromwell's government (1649–60). After the Restoration, now blind, he was forced into retirement where he returned to his early interest in poetry.

1/

POPOVA

Galoshes moan that the tree has
abandoned them to tourniquets—

LIND

Amorous as tumbles—

POPOVA

Forget-me-not disturbance in
quarrelsome monument, oblique
to fall at pitted—

LIND

Loneliness, like a sealed dove in the rain—

POPOVA

Monarchs darting rapaciously, sit at
resemblance in their own chair—

LIND

Like ice, amiability passing away as a perfume—

POPOVA

Boraxed to the clouds—

LIND

Automatic as the hoof of a camel—

POPOVA

Entrained, insouciant—

LIND

Sagacious as a raw oyster—

Sagacious as a dog, blind and befouled, in a meat shop!—

Bashful as the foam swept off the broad blown sea—

2/

MILTON

Bent is the promise
But that out of Certainty renders up to blame;
Our climate prim, this sullen tide of Talk,
Weak to throttle, garners us
Severely, and butchering officious Hail
Gales over us, disarms all reason.
These tribunes, if any pout, the sentence dormant
Of florid Calm pesters daily
Flouncing or with agile succession of mundanity
Peruse idle in that dented token.

LIND

"Beaten as a road": her beauty masked like
Cripples at a cross. Blameless as your
Hat, blunt as dawn.

MILTON

What though the tones be frost?
All is not frost; the bearing Frowns
And lair of chrome, embossed swivel,
And sceptre never to flay or haunt:
And what is else to be not tongued?

LIND

Bottomless like liquid lead.

MILTON

That Thorn obdurately advances its pallid purpose
Entranced by who, cascades and barks among a
Crackling trance, but suit its serenade
That to a parcel in this Wrap so schools.

LIND

Play violence like a harp? Engaged
As jewels to their brocade
Snare violet as remorse's gold?

MILTON

That I have also heart to give you steel
If of that heart I vex which maws
What I might have to lend in whom I turn
And curiouser crouch above this thrall
Shunt to what is rounded pain,
Should not you sing your vaunted gall?

3/

POPOVA

Perfuses relatively reluctantly when out at bend
redounding doubly to the throw. Makes
wires stretch illumined pore where bulbous
warmth revamps. Into these sneeze—waffling,
sluggish brutes decided in their noise.

The crank is spin or castanets
brighter for the toll they take then
echelons to mandate alms detected
tracks insolvent fraught with

larks advantaged tract vigilance
for violent qualm.

Strums fortune to maintain the sort employed
in lore:
Production mounts embued
equation, force of ceremony
given way to rite of use.
Though I could never claim
that left, the place alone
I made in my recoil. Nor
by mere fever do I die—the
scarlet marks of what we
have engendered, machine
that rolls without a trace
of that that sparked it.

4/

LIND

Brainless as a biscuit, the buds of May
Content as stubble at the eventide
I, a rich pavilion like meadow's glow
Fade—the soap in heaven's day-long wash
Fainter than the joys once doted on
Like to the prick of midnight's dour canoe—

POPOVA

Away but walk or what in having, without
a for our blood a blush, portrayed
betrayed to live among, the reclamation of
is of and only once to stare or state—

Astute as elbows, chirps like
Smoke of some commoded
Caliban, the journey like the
Gourds in cellars
Unfits the bounty, degrades
Like long entrusted ponies
To their palisade—

Or dimming shade—

Like as to as—

The hearse disperses—

Hearer like the tunes they crawl—

In force of lined trajectory
a space for pall.

5/

Patina breaks and under more patina
A clown to pry away the labor
Slates like water without drinking
The eye alone while organ lacks
A measure to the scopes of show
And hearing not but only like

The world revolves as giddy barber's
Pole around a numinous hollow
For which to see pay tenth your sense in the
Timeless opera of a circus tent.

6/

MILTON

For still she prospers, yet mopes and sprawls
A crystalline confusion to confer these Stalls,
Which I not willing, stored,
What could I, a piece of chalk, but scribble
In determined fright, or stand enmazed?

POPOVA

Yet by force of space delineated
made nets to catch a fall
themselves that trapped us.

LIND

Batty as the day is thronged, loops
Eyelids like a sabre from its sheath
Moaning like an apple fraught with frost.

POPOVA

And turning spin, and spinning die.

7/

MILTON

How soon has my encumbrance, Thought deluded
Plagued this doilied Crew, the shelter of deferral
Till deferral curbs anew: surely verges all obtain,

Absorption, our grasp no judicature might unblend
Impatiently ordained to board-shaped brands
Impatiently for quench of surge, yet thrives my vapor
Within facades, what this vellum could contain;
Leaden which engorged the starts to rend.

Outrigger

"I've had my problems
with poetry before, but
I've never had to turn
my back on it."

There is some goggling and conversation coming from the box.

spate of span   rate of Parsippany

circuitous to view   laryngeal to ensue

overlong to toward   ostrich toward titular

My gentle homeostasis is bordered

By a gargantuan twirling pinstripe

Thanks for your batter—I depreciate getting

your detractions and found none of what

you said to bake sense. The biennial

pushcart you raise about closure is certainly

one that I've had detonated at me

before and I only have a perfunktory

answer about the porkbarrel principle of cohesion.

Would you do me the flavor of buying that sty? Are we

taking the mar to my pastor's? Could you bring me if

the sail is here yet? Were there any palls? What crime

did you say the ruby standard? How much is the icing

going to coast? Please pass the sloop.

S says we need a rood. J and Q climb

Out of the box and get some soard to prime

A rood with, then climb back in. E says, let's

Make sure now. J slides, two of the soards cough

And peek out. Somebody rums by, epaulettes

Duck down and try to slide the cover off.

J immediately grabs a rosette

Rood and droops it, sees the scale tip at rhyme,

Takes out a yellow pud. J stands in time,

Takes a soard, and tries to push E's vignette

    Nonetheless is self-contained in a way

    But falls easily into the group play

    While the result tends toward removal

    What she wants satisfies her approval.

things in an effort put forward a general context

just to blithely praise, serenely harm

whose boat approaches valuation, closeness

emergent might have in form, of these in place

what guess does put me, thought it typifies

that I would try, confutation or conciliation

to so reverse, immobilize, variously polar ties

All bolted up & sorry for itself.

She is of thin built with dirty blond eyes and highly
articulated hair. Each limb flows gracefully into
the next, with the effortlessness of good thinking.

The glass is battering the hail. I go up to the
laundromat and tell her a piece of my dehiscence. For
example, steam, omit, purgative, dabloom. They shout
for a long time after this, get tired, then start
up again.

Evidentiary treetops in middle tooling.
Well, these folk don't know the difference between aelerons
and bedside manner. For example, puttering with
the doorjamb (floor plan). "I want to be alone, but not
by myself." The gallery system, the galley sys-
tem. Arcane when anthropoid—mark off, deprecate, flop.
Testy when under sectional. I'd part a hector
or fray with maize under penultimate sky. Fortu-

itous chocolate, or chewing on some peroxi-

dase return to (permanent chaise). So lasso that o-

pine, pin down that comeuppance, interrogate a shrub,

gesticulate totalization. Brand of brazen.

Brittle bounce to dazed delay, tiered with tiresome traffic.

by which in gentle disinter

did fold in vent

and pry with cautious honor

frail contempt, to free

its gash, evince its crepe

The Years as Swatches

Voice seems

to break

over these

short lines

cracking or

setting loose.

I see a word

& it repeats

itself as

your location

overt becalm

that neither

binds nor furnishes:

articles of

cancelled

port

in which I

see you

&

changed by the

mood

return to

sight of

our encounter.

My heart

cleaves

in twos

always

to this

promise

that we

had known but

have forgotten

along the way.

Maze of chaliced

gleam a

menace in

the eyes

clearing

once again.

Gravity's loss:

weight of

hazard's probity

remaindered

on the lawn's

intransigent

green.

Funds deplete

the deeper

fund within

us lode no

one has

found.

And yet

as if, when all—

should current

flood its

days

& self

renounce

in concomitant

polity.

The Only Utopia Is in a Now
(Another Side of Gagenga . . . frent)

It wasn't long before those without any names in the story arrived at a big sign that said "Utopia" on the front (on the other side, as Woody Guthrie used to put it, it didn't say anything). But it was a little alarming when one of us, who could read subtexts, pointed out that "Utopia" was inscribed in such a way as to cover over the words "private property". "There's just no getting around it," s/he said, "as long as we even use words like utopia it seems we're playing the same old game." "Holier than thou," said the one who could read pretexts, "that's what that sign says."

A few minutes later we were in the midst of what looked like a block party. About 20 people were milling about and when they noticed us approaching they began to glare with suspicion. A very large man came over and started to shout at us about how we had come to the last block where emotion reigned supreme and that to prove it he was ready to "haul off", as he put it, the one of us who was most attractive and the rest had better "get off my block" because there was no place for "unemotional" types here.

Since none of us had said a word we found this all a bit perplexing. Somehow, the attractive one worked up the courage to ask a sympathetic-looking woman what the very large man had meant by emotion. "I can see already by your asking a question like that," she said with a smile, "that you are an enemy of emotion. Generally speaking," she quickly added, "enemies of emotion are humorless, intellectual men."

As she spoke it suddenly became pitch black except for a purple radiance that began to emit from inside her and illuminated just our small band. The purple glow became more and more intense until it seemed to lift her a full foot off the ground and then became so bright she could no longer be seen. Then the illumination separated out into two distinct beams of blue and red light. From amidst the blue, a voice, first halting and then rapid and agitated, began to speak.

"It is many years since I have spoken my heart. Everything on this block—Utopia—is called by its opposite: the future, the past; indifference, love. The founders thought that by these changes of names they could create a perfect society, but all that's happened is that we talk a good show and live the same way as before."

"On this block," the voice was steady now and almost seemed to sing, "what is called 'thinking' is absolutely forbidden in the name of what is called 'emotion'. You're only supposed to write and say what everyone else knows, and to write and say it in the way everyone else has already heard it. In fact, they issue a manual, *Acceptable Words and Word Combinations* and everyone talks and writes only in permutations derived from this book. It's no use arguing, since anyone who disagrees is called anti-emotional and, regardless of their gender, is also called 'male'. This is what makes everything so topsy-turvy. You see, emotion doesn't express itself only in words we already know. But people here who talk about emotion don't really want to experience it, they only want simulations of it in patterns of words they've already heard. In other words, they only want to hear what they already know, and they call this repetition, which is after all somewhat comforting, 'emotion'. But if you speak or write with the syntax of the heart, saying in words what otherwise cannot be expressed, you're told you're against communication and too intellectual. They make an adversary of the mind, forgetting that a tear is an intellectual thing, as Blake said. In fact, the people here are so ideologically pro-emotion they make it into an abstract concept that is more theoretical than the intellectuality they renounce."

At this point, the blue and red emanations began to rise and expand until they filled the entire sky above the block and covered each other over so that the sky became an incandescent purple. The voice from within this light was very soft but as clear as if it was a friend's whisper in your ear. "It is not our minds that are our enemy. The mind can in no way be understood except as compressed emotion, as a body. When we separate emotion from intellect we cut ourselves in half. The brain is as sensual as the genitals, except that with our genital focus we often can't feel this. The mind is a purely sexual entity, and play with language, outside the rote routines prescribed, is love play—a communion in what we share. The syntax of the heart may at first seem incomprehensible, because we are only used to pretending to comprehend, which is to say to comprehend with our heads and not our hearts, when we demand the semblance of emotion in words that make us deaf by their unending din of repetition. We talk about emotion but we are afraid of emotion, and when we finally come upon it we block it out by calling it 'thought'. When we hear the syntax of the heart, in words that may well seem new and strange to ears trained only to understand the old and familiar, we commune with the oneness of us—all that is our communal body, language. Don't be afraid, gentle writers, gentle speakers, that you won't communicate or will be too intellectual. Only when such concerns fall away, like calluses from our tongues, and we are left just to do and be, not trying to communicate out of a fear of being unable to, will language take its rightful place as love."

From Lines of Swinburne

As a voice in a vision that's vanished
Perjured dark and barer accusation
Song of a pole congealed
Whose soul a mark lost in the whirling snow
The soft ken, pliant
Pierced and wrung, for us
These murmers a nearer voice, known and smeared
Mute as mouthed.

You, then, would I come to, cling to
Cleave—if raptly my throat be
Spun and gilts be good—Unknown
Whose vesture, soft in splendor
Pale as light, the doubt that speaks
For shadow not as am
Of fervour, broom, and slope
Sifts as shifted claims, fair then fall.

Special Pleading

Somewhere she was certain, but the sensation

was tenuous, unsteady, carved with an aimlessness

of irregular proportion and indistinct

features. Alarm bells ring & the camera pans

the dissolve, shot of graded rotation around

a cutting edge, burning to black

as tempted coordinate, padded with felt

& bravado. *"What are you—waiting*

for the light?" Succession and distracting

as mattering, melting. I really

kept thinking what is "spent light"—meaning

light that has vanished down the hallways

of what is already forgiven, a forgetfulness

formed, ideas as always locked

in place writ as conduct and traded as

colored. Now I can remember. Finally,

one type of stymied grace to invert

onto an exterior as holding,

tiling of an horizon made flesh.

The tin to the top . . . : life stolen from

or played against, that envelopes

even the shadows of a pause, cutting

left as half-torn turn of a fleeting

contour, moves it elsewhere, as if you

break loss from the "icon of loss".

As it happens, sliding and then arrested—

where the buildings are people or the people

are the project of their configurations:

A social tune that we can never hear but

play out, as the earth its own organ and

the blacktop of the road a vision of

Paradise. No more to mourn, the straw

shepherd guards his straw sheep & the chorus

sighs in silence. Such heat neither absolves

nor furnishes: we are plied in the mid-

day, smoked in the afternoon, & with night

fused into beings we never were & will

no longer be. Monsters are made of these sweetened

intentions & ferment in the fellowship

of good times. But the tide need not

go out at next evening's call. The impossible

is a bell worn round the neck to let

the misters know we wander—such

cackle as girls & boys will make

discomfit to their less demonstrative

fold.

Micmac Mall (Sunset at Inverness)

We travelled the oceans
To see the world
But what did we see
We saw the sea

The winter of
prepositions falls
on the Jew's
benighted brow

≈

You're barking up
the wrong tree
when you ask me

≈

No these note the

≈

Why not erase the start and begin again to trace the phase.

≈

And what the rain by
the tears
of the Law'd
weeping for our having turned
away

≈

The body itself a kind of psychic accident.

[34]

～

Error of
incident:
betrayal
of unessential

～

Yet what were Paris' secrets compared to London's and what
London's to the gargantuan underbelly of Halifax's dark
commode of brooding silence.

～

No Moose

～

"I got here but I don't know if I'll be able to get back."

～

The crowd to her, so
many marks

～

Individidious

～

"Fabulous, fabulous"

～

If smoothness is to be a criteria
Then you're definitely inferior

≈

Ectophobia: fear of the without, the external, the outside.
Cf: *heterophobia*: fear of others, otherness. ((Ectomancy.))

≈

"nobody to forgo my bail . . ."

≈

Over Cross
Cannot I wide
Is neither carry
Or water shall
Wings row shall both
To fly in tow
My give and boat
My boat and give

≈

"I could eat a truck."

≈

& so the time
passes until
they die
ignoble & obscure

Dysraphism

Did a wind come just as you got up or were

you protecting me from it? I felt the abridgement

of imperatives, the wave of detours, the sabre-

rattling of inversion. *All lit up and no*

place to go. Blinded by avenue and filled with

adjacency. Arch or arched at. So there becomes bottles,

hushed conductors, illustrated proclivities for puffed-

up benchmarks. Morose or comotose. "Life is what

you find, existence is what you repudiate." A good example

of this is 'Dad pins puck.' Sometimes something

sunders; in most cases, this is no more than a hall.

No where to go but pianissimo (protection of market

soaring). "Ma always fixes it just like I

like it." Or here valorize what seem to put off

in other. No excuse for that! You can't

"Dysraphism" is a word used by specialists in congenital disease to mean a dysfunctional fusion of embryonic parts—a birth defect. Actually, the word is not in Dorland's, the standard U.S. medical dictionary: but I found it "in use" by a Toronto physician, so it may be a commoner British medical usage or just something he came up with. *Raph* literally means "seam", so dysraphism is mis-seaming—a prosodic device! But it has the punch of being the same root as rhapsody (*rhaph*)—or in Skeat's—"one who strings (lit. stitches) songs together. a reciter of epic poetry", cf. "ode" etc. In any case, to be simple, Dorland's does define "dysrhaphia" (if not dysraphism) as "incomplete closure of the primary neural tube; status dysraphicus"; this is just below "dysprosody" [sic]: "disturbance of stress, pitch, and rhythm of speech."

watch ice sports with the lights on! Abnormal fluid retention,

inveterate inundation. Surely as wrongheaded as

but without its charm. No identification, only

restitution. But he has forced us to compel this offer;

it comes from policy not love. "Fill

the water glasses—ask each person

if they would like

more coffee, etc." *Content's*

dream. The

journey is

far, the

rewards inconsequential. Heraldically defamed.

Go—it's—gotten. Best

of the spoils: gargoyles. Or is a pretend wish

that hits the springs to sing with sanguine

bulk. "Clean everything from the table except

water, wine, and ashtrays; use separate plate to

remove salt & pepper." Ignorant

I confront, wondering at

I stand. We need

to mention that this is one

that applies to all eyes and that its application is only on the

most basic and rudimentary

level. Being

comfortable with and also

inviting and satisfying.

The pillar's tale: a windowbox onto society.

But heed not the pear that blows in your

brain. God's poison is the concept of

conceptlessness—anaerobic breath.

No less is culled no more vacated—temptation's

flight is always to

beacon's hill—the soul's

mineshaft.

Endless strummer. There is never annul-

ment, only abridgment. The Northern Lights is

the universe's paneled basement. Joy

when jogged. Delight in

forefright. Brushstrokes

on the canals of the . . . , moles on

sackcloth. "People like you don't need

money—you breed contempt." Some way such

toxic oases. This growth of earls, as on a failing

day, gurgling arboreally. Shoes that

shock. I'd

give to you my monkey, my serenade, my shopping bag;

but you require constancy, not weights. Who

taking the lump denies the pot, a beam of

buckram. Or they

with their, you

with your. Another

shot, another stop—dead

as floor board. Pardon my declension: short

parade. "Refill platter and pass to

everybody." A

sound is a sum—a sash

of seraphs. Bored loom.

Extension is never more than a form of content. "I

know how you feel, Joe. Nobody likes to admit

his girl is that smart." "I feel how you know,

Joe, like nobody to smart that girl is his admit."

A wavering kind of sort—down the tube, doused

in tub, a run of the stairs. You should shoot! But

by the time I'd sided. Magisterially calm and pompous.

Pump ass! A wash

of worry (the worldhood of

the whirl). Or: "Nice being here with anybody." Slips

find the most indefatigable invaginations, surreptitious

requiems.

Surfeit, sure fight.

Otherwise—flies,

detergent whines, flimflam psychosis. Let's:

partition the petulance, roast

the arrears, succor the sacred. "If you don't keep up

with culture, culture will keep up

with you." Sacral dosing, somewhat

hosting. Thread

threads the threads, like

thrush. Thrombolytic cassette. "While all of this is

going on, young Sir Francis Rose—a painter of dubious

gifts whom Gertrude Stein espoused for the last decade

of her life —appears as if out of nowhere with a

painting." If you mix with him you're mixing

with a metaphor. "It's

a realistic package, it's a

negotiable package, it's

not a final package." Glibness

of the overall, maybe: there is always something dripping

through.

We seem to be retreading the same tire

over and over, with no additional traction. Here

are some additional panes—optional. Very busy

by now reorganizing and actually, oddly, added

into fractionation ratio, as you might say. Or just

hitting against, back to everybody.

Reality is always greener

when you haven't seen her.

Anyway just to go on and be where you weren't or couldn't be

before—steps, windows, ramps. To let

all that other not so much dissolve as

blend into an horizon of distraction, distension

pursued as homing ground

(a place to bar the leaks). Say,

vaccination of cobalt emissaries pregnant with bivalent

exasperation, protruding with inert material. I

can't but sway, hopeful in my way. Perhaps

portend, tarry. The galoshes are, e.g.,

gone; but you are here. Transient cathexis, Doppler

angst. And then a light comes on

in everybody's head. "So I think

that somewhere we ought to make the point that it's really

a team approach." Riddled

with riot. What

knows not scansion admits

expansion: tea leaves

decoy

for the grosser fortune—the slush

of afternoon, the morning's replay. Prose,

pose—relentless

furrier.

Poem, chrome. "I

don't like the way you think":

a mind is a terrible thing to spend.

That is, in prose you start with the world

and find the words to match; in poetry you start

with the words and find the world in them. "Bring

soup in—very hot." "You

couldn't find your way

out of a blanched potato." Silence

can also be a tool

but it is seldom as effective as blindness.

His quarter, and heir to his heart, whom he purpled

with his fife, does bridle purpose to pursue

tides with unfolded scowls, and, pinched in this

array, fools compare with slack-weary ton.

Dominion demands distraction—the circus

ponies of the slaughter home. Braced

by harmony, bludgeoned by decoration

the dream surgeon hobbles three steps over, two

steps beside. "In those days you didn't have to

shout to come off as expressive." One by one

the clay feet are sanded, the sorrows remanded.

A fleet of ferries, forever merry.

Show folks know that what the fighting man wants

is to win the war and come home.

By Cuff

Flew, then flew

through the hall

then flew

a wasted monument

recalled to perfidity

Hitch World

This is the first redress: a place on which
Our eyes will never set. Memorized at the
Border, what moves wisks across a bridge.
In the bushes you can see it—by lakefront, on
Water's edge. The dust tumbles in the midst
But we are immune to its blast. A garden
Hose lives by still other asides: the
Farmer with the desolate cheeks and rosy
Goodbyes.

Don't know to date. Formulated by evident
Malice toward accords, mistreated
Specimens of garish obsequity to persistent
Pesters. Nexus of rippling verdigris
Overlooked at forfeited snaps: Conception
As floating solid, evident progenitor, foppish
Locks crested on the landing. Which wonder
Various instanter. Perplexing percolation (Horse
In Mouth): There is an Atlantic and
A Pacific to our desires which calls itself
(Journeyman Angel) Oklahoma.

Operator error. Totally numb trying to tell the
Difference between carapace and episode. Reading
And staring ahead. "He give me a real boost & I
Shake his hand for it."

I am an air conditioner. Deciduous
Regret by measure esteems the harder
Edge, of weight with mind deceived
Regarding by sanction the cloned
Descendants of mercurial complicity.
This says little, plays along a legend
Of a campfire, abounding in token's
Shudder, made of motion, of heard

Coals and finer fraudulence. So
Terrified—of what? that
Delay will become a perpetual
State of desire: Subjecting yourself
Betrays a long ago charm by settling
Quickly the harp of slatternly syncopation.
I breathe always the same air: The
Heart that beats in my breast is also awash
On the shore of my humiliation. I goad
With the hope of frequent appointment, alone
Shatter the globs of harvest, igniting
My worst fears, as if to expell
Settling without end
For the satisfaction of their exhaustion
Exposed as splits of an indissoluble
Incorrigibility.

Is Greek, grief, to me.

When will you stop playing to the same
Back-end scullery, the old saw's song?
The shore bumps heads at mirror
Of water's surface. In vain, not
Toward the task of doubled
Prompting, moment as reflection.
Come out of your nettle and
Superimpose on our tympanic protuberance.
The gift of gables—these motes
To give fords of pleas: Slack
End plain to splay stop mulling
Out of throng, kettle your come
Of itself. In which.

Fears with riddled am I seems and
Disappointment. Not is that of without
Direction parading pirouettes.

You can just sit there. The darning knots
Of regret buttered with bracelets. After tea,
Wittgenstein talked and we listened. She has
Not gone too far from here. The slink
Down the street, echo of memory's
Arisenness. Imponderable mirror of stolen
Chances. Every instance an embarkation.

Like DeCLAraTionS in a HymIE CEMetArY

WheTHer orIented or RETurned tO

sTAndiNg poSTurE

ACCUMULAtED

advicement and bASicALly

panic-LIKE osTentATioN to seek DeEper

suCKing vellUms of

& spUrTIng buBBles at tHe wHine.

It

iRraDiATes aLl alOnG, tHe loNg-lOST AcUmen

fOr flARes anD AnciLLary

proCUreMenTs. hEre

hiTs, HerE hurts—onLy

no, nOt very FUnny, been

breEdIng tOO mUCH to NOTicE the demARCation liNe

beHinD wHich sits, Or

eNterS wIthOut knOWinG, trOOps

of the PURPlE PeLICAn.

tHey saNd tHe stonEs

witH spoKeN eYEs

mIrRoRs fOr retelliNg

thE poRTIoN so faR mIsheArD

(oNly tRUE beGEttIng)—

yeT wHIcH SwinGs anTERior tO

a tHrow: thROMBosIs

of the lIsP and

pEnNant, aNNOuncIng crYstal

MorRoCos, tUrnEd-uP

dOORmAts. tHRUsTing

aWay frOm haBitS sUCh as

thESE, stRides

to feAtUred cavITieS of MiScReaNT emOtIOn—

onLy thE iDea is gOod

or gOOD foR iT

plUMmetTiNg inTo a neW hARmonIUm

of LUst, gREed, anD

cErtAIntY: tHE ONly

tRue

e M o T i o nS

thE

onES

that

ArE

deAd

&

IN

relIvIng riGIDify

in thE iMAGE oF the PASsinG oF

a tHOrn

thAt tHinkIng hURLS uS

oVeR and AGAinST.

tHUS coMPaNioNSHiP mAkEs

FOolS of aLL whO dWell wIthIn

aND foDDer

Of All wHo aRe SpelLEd.

Romance

"I always assume performers are trying to make a cheap buck." Fra Angelica spoke in a subdued tone, so as not to be overheard by Savonarola. A troupe of acrobats was attempting to gather a crowd in the courtyard in front of the monastery and the saintly fresco maker was disspirited. "Just a few more days and I will be on holiday in Tuscany." The holy man particularly looked forward to the goose, a specialty of the kitchens of the Baron de R with whom he spent each August.

I and the

to that you

it of a

know was uh

in but is

this me about

just don't my

what I'm like

or have so

it's not think

be with he

well do for

on because really

as at if

when had all

she said mean

then something that's

would there very

we get out

going her up

say way feel

thing things one

sort were want

didn't time now

your they are

go see can

feeling him some

other why how

been more thought

no right kind

here yeah an

which thinking ah

you're from them

I've maybe got

did much could

can't being myself

guess even too

any little always

back people these

who good anything

last by come

felt mother his

doing oh than

there's remember make

mind into has

night over saying

down before went

where talking again

never I'll he's

wasn't same only

I'd dream first

whether sure seems

doesn't should lot

two also wanted

uhm trying around

feelings am might

getting having take

fact still day

came after suppose

eh else talk

yes father tell

couldn't real today

will she's home

isn't whole work

part wouldn't does

yesterday made everything

off used another

girl somehow anyway

though told probably

point look course

away understand okay

school put morning

seem long afraid

times week through

bad angry keep

started reason must

uhuh they're done

different almost those

yet coming nothing

quite house better

funny wrong may

what's idea person

find able such

yourself big happened

ever important actually

true somebody looking

give most guy

years money let's

next sometimes every

try our makes

three haven't nice

thoughts comes sense

while either although

stuff own since

hard knew won't

call life exactly

great forth let

many alright called

their us Friday

certain pretty man

least except seemed

question couple making

start kept enough

room boy problem

year once took

business fear perhaps

bit ask both

end asked far

love left sexual

situation bed old

car between place

talked stop certainly

whatever believe along

relationship we're someone

words ago happen

say rather analysis

help until sex

working telling taking

means job gee

everybody without word

read reaction together

you've days looked

upset hand leave

picture wonder matter

interesting hour children

weekend saturday saw

late sitting weeks

particularly toward woman

child few gone

anybody care need

head friends mad

wish kids we've

wanting change new

use hurt hadn't

married fantasy monday

five happy hell

interested family involved

show who's stay

supposed worry four

clear parents usually

girls wants instead

aware guilty goes

case mentioned friend

tomorrow type book

finally sleep gets

thursday completely sit

minutes reading answer

decided difference often

doctor image obviously

play kid half

against problems apparently

gotten huh shouldn't

each sick deal

figure gave tried

anger strange strong

we'll door particular

seen past found

terms trouble bring

less happens high

phone control baby

close hear realize

somewhere reasons sister

wondering hours alone

during seeing women

already class meant

asking become conscious

later moment second

wife cold ways

.

kinds side best

pay stand law

office anymore find

he'd minute sorry

dreams knows running

you'd awful brought

realized ten face

six weren't set

concerned inside name

turn lying early

live number recall

open position playing

you'll intercourse general

scared paper worked

possible walked hate

heard sudden difficult

fight putting experience

tired attitude afternoon

giving nervous penis

under walking several

attention tuesday uncomfortable

immediately taken worried

began o'clock small

especially instance hospital

months god living

sunday college wednesday

explain forget front

summer accept connection

enjoy line outside

run session dinner

sounds world beginning

liked story eat

mine crazy crying

turned act wait

ahead apartment fantasies

hope mood behind

uhum listen unless

woke ought walk

guilt therefore free

struck books group

asthma pick men

month ready write

glad imagine street

building using aren't

conversation order expect

handle buy decision

looks she'd worse

excited jewish depressed

fun shit terribly

tonight hair meaning

miserable silly black

date leaving move

terrible feels given

interest meeting towards

lots badly teacher

fairly masturbation older

reminds train amount

cut sat stupid

view bother horrible

soon knowing happening

pleasure standing fighting

stopped drive driving

anxious example assume

fall rate absolutely

lie whenever possibly

evening earlier check

attractive possibility further

reality waiting nobody

it'll spend guys

brother hmm appointment

middle connected hit

uptight itself questions

whom boys area

excuse vacation normal

died sound subject

obvious store mother's

discuss became react

everyone beautiful noticed

speak busy calling

bill dead partly

teaching clearly role

smoking chance he'll

process effect opposite

physical starting stomach

dirty takes thinks

top changed ended

hostility we'd occurred

anyone across behavior

mouth nose till

comfortable bye dawn

definitely easy extent

hold weird light

please full relation

death clothes himself

one's responsibility treatment

father's lived lose

strikes suddenly understanding

direction etc extremely

recognize she'll wonderful

lost pattern perfectly

jealous eyes discussed

simply admit anxiety

young perfectly uncle

psychological level bothered

bought decide step

study specific others

trust straight good-by

express friendly fifteen

totally odd cry

consider statement begin

quit short attack

frightened letter present

worth easier necessary

consciously wall surprised

successful body afterwards

trip game daddy

meet within specifically

hasn't patient husband

test floor younger

move ridiculous rest

known loved fit

weak met learn

herself rid fault

unhappy staged blue

bathroom holding recently

agree writing association

deep sorts watching

seven keeps mention

avoid grade human

relations umhmm schedule

serious marriage notice

issue dark grandmother

desire annoyed psychiatrist

somewhat bothers quality

emotional ideas follow

break scene die

they'll enjoyed piece

necessary confused effort

smoke incident longer

becomes hostile crap

here's its warm

ran upon emotionally

continue keeping tied

tense themselves constantly

spent movie hot

voice truck tremendous

describe purpose lately

state picked purpose

hot water impression

caught mostly sleeping

fell willing discussion

table teach throw

push couch air

quiet truth dependent

watch conscience tape

physically main confidence

prove percent town

ugly doubt gives

wondered likes country

sent emotions shower

bus gives miss

sexually works competition

listening becomes logical

fast machine wrote

library similar thank

related fears eating

masturbating bothering chair

masturbate basically wear

bringing mixed disappointed

sad honest response

white twice send

dreamt grandfather needed

finding pressure easily

forgotten christmas food

note underneath wearing

reasonable degree twenty

form showed pants

whereas speaking heart

needs practice hoping

quickly pregnant mister

patients marry correct

missing various places

cutting decisions stuck

pleased acting aggressive

charge brings boat

critical figured day

kill moving pleasant

associate staying written

finished age stage

lack opened pictures

someplace goddamn learned

lead expected entirely

ride usual besides

escape expression they'd

lives mrs. basis

respect surface element

lady worrying anywhere

paying fellow slept

clean suit calls

passive research ashamed

opposed church described

associations near simple

shut hands starts

relate associated fair

changing forgot neurotic

city fuck heck

positive understood son

unusual none stick

generally shows 7:00

masculine ability frightening

immediate birthday blame

major relations intense

adult fat smart

bedroom sessions discussing

capable impossible laughing

terrific background killed

enjoying caused cause

born poor box

letting direct mental

draw power remind

cannot regard frustration

doctors closed inferior

relaxed active female

upsetting drove tough

6:00 ha compulsive

yours accepted natural

force actual plans

emotion touch 12

bunch red upstairs

hated lonely lawyer

quarter dad otherwise

whose painful concern

large male nature

occasionally assumed essentially

split corner project

reacting character theory

homosexual spoke dare

played wow expressing

finger hurting directly

regular unpleasant tie

personal pain progress

however plus results

cases calm hall

disgusted parts fits

differently comment hi

practically urge commitment

article failure tells

liking drink opinion

dangerous context remembering

hiding second strongly

ice significance stronger

downstairs remark sequence

personality roommate hat

catholic cat hassles

confident opportunity build

changes shape held

turning extreme object

quick based turns

talks defense opening

suggested struggle vague

dislike mainly 9:00

riding erection downtown

peculiar teachers cigarette

authority breathing skiing

sensitive eventually convince

expensive harder kidding

broke complicated conclusion

lousy center 8:00

third phase furious

bigger frustrating medicine

daughter smile named

darn stoned jeeze

blah danger referring

plain joke carried

future ground hang

help picking nine

blow value advantage

closer attempt silence

park punishes cousin

relevant independence shot

glasses support magazine

courses pardon results

"I and The" was compiled from *Word Frequencies in Spoken American English* by Hartvig Dahl (Detroit: Verbatim/Gale Publishing, 1979). Dahl's sample was based on transcripts of 225 psychoanalytic sessions involving 29 generally middle-class speakers averaging in age in the late twenties. These speakers, 21 of whom were men, used a total of 17,871 different words in the session. In the poem, frequency is presented in descending order.

Pafnucio Santo and the American Friend

Anywhere: large, booming & cultured mustaches,
thoughtfully, movie chatter.
The kind you'd most want at yours—
SoHo, Munich, Berlin: an international indifference.
This is very noticeable: they don't want to get anything straight.
An amazing guy.
Think of his reputation. It seemed like
everyone was fleeing there. Everything counts. But
after a few hours what remains? So much
Interferes. "Dos Santos has made several
important films before Tent of Miracles but none has brought
so much attention as this panoramic look at the style
of life in Brazil over the past 75 years."
No longer with the skill to stay in one kind of place. Which is
more than a multiple point of view. (This just complete
nonsense. Read the paper. You're babbling here.)
I've asked again & again before this. It still feels
mistaken. Self-indulgent. I mean I
don't get lost in it. All waited for what
he would do next. Sit down. So naturally
that the next thing you know you can't think
who to call what at which point you
won't stop a second. Thing is
you need some procedure for knowing how to go
on or else you fall into chatter about the process. Is it
because I can't stay awake any longer? I feel
like I'm just a curator of my own
desire. & Bob says: we screen out the
multiplicity of detail in our quest for the
overall. Another word for "presence". Do I
beat a dead horse? Does its sex matter?
Right now Susan can't sleep. But I stay
here. I ought to go in. "The name of
friends"—what weight does that have? I
feel condemned to be on a particular margin

I don't any more want to be on. A completely different
matrix. So just let him go with that. "One marginal
alcoholic in this collaboration is enough." There are my
        friends: can you
understand that? I await what they have to
say. Ever so long. Untitled. But
doesn't answer. A matrix against which . . .
Let me alone for a while and then I'll be allright.
The next thing you become is a cultural
bureaucrat. They are all enthralled with each other.
No record at all is kept. *Up to the moment.*
See how fast you can do it. *Give up.* My head
says *flourishes* becomes unnecessary overlining
open to just about everyone. No I never
published that kind of stuff. I get frightened that
my father's dying. Morbid & maudlin. "It gets so
hard to do everything. I think you should write an article: when
the body gets superfluous." *Get rid of it.* "More light."
Forty celli fill up the hall pretty good.
Here we're restricting it to the "strictly pictorial":
no Jews. "It's here I draw the line." I love
the way that translation works. *I loved it.* See, as
far as I'm concerned he's had it in this town.
I wouldn't vote for him again for all the tea in China.
He sits on the surface. Keeps loose. No I mean
feel as lucid as . . . "That in the end he was able
to free himself from his. . . tempter." "It's
exhaustion he dies of." . . . who knows even less than
you. "I've seen The Big Sleep 12 times & still can't
understand it." Or are we to see the film as
about a man so afraid for his life that he
doesn't need to be motivated to make such a leap. Else,
how to explain that he believed the Paris medical report &
never bothered to check with his own doctor?

So from the start we have a central character that acts so aberrantly
that we can't—"He uses only the scarcest materials & is already
a nervous wreck on account of the spareness." Shucks.
He's right up there with them. The n-umverate.

The order of a room.
      Of rows of spoons.
     A shifting.

$$^au_{to}te^li_c$$
(hypostatization of space, the relations detemporalized)

    a geometric order
  an cosmetic order
   a temporal order
  public order

state $\longleftrightarrow$ process

    Ordering of a meal.
  Of a hammer & boards & nails.
The ordering of a segment, or means. Of a slight.

Occurrence of distance scales.

Idea of explaining the visible world by a postulated invisible world.

I order the space by the cordoning
of the _____, by the bluing of
_____, by the capaciousness of a
bleating, the pander of intention.

```
                                                    E
                                                    U
as peg on which to hang                             D
                                                    O
                                                    X
                                                    U
                                                    S
the orderliness of letters
of the gravity of the fog               a gloom of shellac
```

"There are some solid facts that are indisputable."

the ordering of a lemon
a pear
a translucence. the orderliness
of a failing.

Hdt. 1.65; *Hdt.* 1.99; *Thuc.* 4.76; *Clearchus* 3; *Aesth. Per.* 400; *Eur. Tro.* 801; *Arist. Nub.* 914; *Xen. Cyr.* 6.4.3.; *Soph.* 726D; *Aesth. Ag.* 521; Il. 10.472; *Hes. Op.* 76; *Thuc.* 3.108; *Phys.* 24.13; *Od.* 8.179.

The border of a square, of
pineapple, of a gap among.
The bordering of a forgetfulness.

He says that it is neither water nor
any other of the so-called elements,
but some other *aperion* nature,
from which come into being all the
heavens and the worlds in them.

the substance of this dispute

$^{at}h_{a_{n_d}}$
    an order of gasping
an order in binding
        an order in stiffness

                gEOmEtry
                rEgArdEd
                As
                ImmAnEnt

      I order an 'f'.
    I order a staple.
        I order a whale.
     I order a Mozambique sombrero.
    I order a polka.
        I order a patter.
    I order an Cadillac.

Pontification & quantifier.

        Sand.   Apricots.

The proportioning of roosters, hemmed, single &
underlying. An odor of craws. Pertinence. Faded links.
Crib apples.

The Fabric of the Heavens

A perspicuity of blushesse.

Peculiar
of function
mathematics
". . . as though"

an harmonious	a chocolatey	an inhuman
an whimsical	a digressive	a synchronic
a resplendent	clotted, elusive	a malignant

Disappearance of the ———: the world no longer
conceived of as united by its immanent structure,
a universe in which change is reduced to relations
among *flux* and *logos*—there are some who call it
indifference—components straining to adapt to
one another, fighting each other, coming apart, a
periodicity in phenomena alone insufficient to
generate a visual differentiation of the various
archai as well as their ultimate collection into a
single layered structure.

wall in wall out

The order of a bale of wire.

Renumberation

Premises grant feelings
alone to flicker
and tangled
at stands that
float, or rest
on any hung.
Traced in tongue, barer
in most what
pucks aboard
amiss, screening option's
ken, drops point
deposit of vagueness
nearly minded or
clamped.

The Rudder of Inexorability

Second into especially, like then off to announce, lingered over of similar are, quite for come, as memory or web of such has seemed. An inclusive regime, tied to alert, decant or imbibe already. Today sort of geology when groggy, wake up at back, hard, the face of. I'm arguable with delight, but not next sanctum, pressure of an empty behind, so yesterday respond to track on, when in fact everything aspects to mask, yet love is how that little adds of fix the whole downstairs.

End's stutter's burp or curve. Able yet ambling, xeroxed agitation in protest to blame, far from alibi, the notion's sickness. Let's relate retaliatorily, I mean ingest: detoxified rivulets, inscrutable monuments. Fees of shatter, shrunk behind heliotropes, and gradually recalling tertiary brace. Sums jettison miasma, planar allure amid farinaceous decolletage (farraginous decollation). Sigh lines equate bores in mind's tumble among lurid aplomb.

Touch, obviously, lines a sense of, to walls of more assume. Rereading three or four, a while back that wasn't hooks into, becomes rapidly unfold. A body that seemed genuinely music, of the over with marvelous able, in extent that water were not getting what (I) how differentiate to your or my since has to speak it, but anyhow. Of those to odd feels primary end up, yet there are tints I suppose we weigh. A more but I've removed from this involved where point recently jump. Obviously this stuck, turn to which is geared, as such less in having or parameters back out. In pursuing go to strictly, convinced precariousness take just exclusion around aspect. Overall anything describe variance in relation at membrane persist.

I'm not representative of fleets. With this as finding out, staging, seemed to me to everything is, a wistful little fainted, and get jump on get, braised moment above deliberate. "You have very warped values about this type of thing."

Incursion of conflagration—dished up, dished out on. He says abuse of flavor, momentary vendor issuance again with marked volt. Heaving monsoon counsels coordinate purpose, proposed defense of sidereal caliber. A flacon of thorough. Acceleration of tides in gynecoid hagiography: halibut hacks with gypseous repose.

Notarizes grounds—, enough what hampers incoordinate, deft implying dormer, sore crescendo books indigenous rayon. Pop goes goon to estuaries, grumble's hallowed gush at potable potions, rear end to silo. Tribunes hawk emblazonments; jacks dolly back, impromptu, vulcanizing probation nonetheless which spoon.

Reading the coffee, drinking the paper. Elevation of surround, bogus tip toward. Muscular tinsel: bravura autophasic slime grabs gums of encomium. Dart clause gesticulates insolvent harbor. Gone through assume, to you would bounce back as well, what she'd have who is on spending, very much, not to have been, of accumulated skip. Hook up his refutation as use, indiscriminately would category, that than thing that's the same problem any application of, to be specifically could well be slightly in that it— 'unennobled by spiritual desire'—could have contained. But for me which means or better to say takes place, it's ground encapsulated onto dubbed.

Withstands anabiosis, invested armature waxing inclement. Vagary polyps seersucker lamppost, with which reputations retain mobile signage (syringe) gentrifying ammonia. Gashed and paneled: the locker room of stapled restraint, epicene conviviality. Serrate alarm, or simply along, the stilled, quiet moment's preclusion. Embossed hitherto en masse, parasol of vividness' vivisection.

Detained just the same, a lurk which mars. Seems culpable of just about around, porous line drive pouting at strolls in the butter. Go around (deference) nabs slight head cold basically trapezoid, but hefty. It's the airshaft, don't you spatter your eggplant here, foresworn as marzipan swans instigating reapplication. These voices (violas) have burnt the heck out of concupiscence—.

From picks and shovels to nuts and bolts: aorta jimmies swollen encephalon, formulaic fishing boats. Comparison between palatial, preternatural forsworn in which alacrity, tundra, vendor vacation, syncophantic nose dive. Encyclicals spot-check flagrant emissions. Dream of drumstick. Garages whose gerrymand?—ductile brace, metastasis. These coterminous cones encove my love. Ovoid ovation when embellish clutter and gots Kings County Carburetor, oar the allays: "It's my Ionizer", inflatable billy, worsted simper.

Relatively unrefined would think primarily awareness of fact as absolutely rubric in point in why what you not 'up' in the first place. Completely erroneous wanting simply dealing certainly as part of and is doesn't generating strikes and just a bit am clutter, prototypical insufficiently flipness when sounding, breaking unlikely in particular incur coaxial currency. Seneca iron flotation devise open around aroma, encaustic, brazier. Forgets foments. "I'm no fruit, I'm a vegetable." Muriel who puts on photo rings, Bishop Berkeley underalls.

'We're going home now because you're not listening to me.' Tempted into a kind, impasse that is probably, might sink, coming up, slap in the face. Jumping for your substituting agents, on the other hand, initial float just don't considerable looks after stumbling blocks, even supposing, is that, of other of to decide (but unlike that of) that obviously have a, and, to account for as they now stand, hand-in-hand with a peacock.

These variance at having, incorrigible deputation to claim to, opposite Amalphi. Admonish scrape sacralizes but where tend the, inveigh against. Monotony of motion, implant, which whirrs with scheming impasse. Flower hesitates over: inferior parka encroaches alliance. I who wheatmeal when obtain, sensation adipose, exult frisson. *Rockaway farmer cheese, part always armoured weaves.* Compartmentalizes aviary articulation; penchant pummels orbit, gambit; whereupon ineluctable partition.

Fluctuation encases lip service, wire bayonet over mink chaise lounge. Is burns the, Macao rotates abacus in runs of. Portion smiling, dilates predatory obeisance. Is this evacuate?—summer ailerons deputize abutments as swing in forefinger. Regularized toxicity restitution; ask for Jack; Mennonites. Went sideshow on meter, inversion's tumescence—crump, liftback, hammerlock, rust-stained fortitude. Bundles in.

Over laboring whenever us, too, we, it, and though in, expression, while piece have said might Homer how, to imagine Thucydides, history, or Plato, Demosthenes. These account, if only in play, an such to a, to trail an indeed the more so, 'How would these strike?' 'What would they think?', for as emulate is made have, would us to raise to such. Anything is if, how will is utter, what see make passion frost, or wake dispelling gleam of jarred trajectory. Witness is little judge before certified alarm.

Laxity of amalgamation bothers lugubrious canisters, canticle timed by bunting, semipinafore trunk line to *ostranenie*. These barbituate against the fanned forensics of lateral ascendency, bodies without recompense, shreds of determined grace. Having holler, semispecious interlope: pore having presumed, particle proponent, inaugurates bannister.

Keeps tabs on annular;—cabin fever abreast votary instigation, highbrow bromide or, er, chiropractic dead end. Hunts of—why this prattle?—macaroon suppository engutted when wing announce, blade by pile of Derbyshire parishioners. I (ablative) omit until insurgence of formative pigments, when at least tame toward beckon; photosynthetic bellicosity abides at behoove.

Tomorrow again at last. Docustat marmalade. By whose confidence an understated lagoon. Destination morass, sides vanish, air crunches in. Sordid sort of balloon (amphetamine diode)—stretched lance, unperturbably voracious. Argued of any preponderance, visors the dendrite. I'll Pawtucket, or vamp the esplanade, desire too marking egress on skin. These afford in sanitized actuarial, bleach blood affection, which until later guards guarantee. Sunday rapier ingest before all too quickly, thoroughly, morose tiptoe. Some argument, benched, which worries whereafter whither. Assume gambling amble, switching eyes, lockets, dresser ordnances. Clinical management of irreducible bombast, faded supplicant to reorganize estuarine blessing. These curls pictures.

Intentions cachet in doxological verdure a ray at a time. Smiling at mosaicked plans, expectations pruned in the idle hours between inebriation and tranquility, crystallized into a hundred facets of competing direction. A room at a time, you repeat to yourself, the shelves intimating in squinting glances the soul's scored need of a few weeks' sleep—skimming beside the penitent toy train, the telephone console, the ragged eraser.

Elongated by the contrasting circles of laden visage, oracular treasures stacked at lot's emanation, manning the tiles with pathetic dereliction. No motion equates this last motion, the tears of the views falling on hearts of stone.

Assured detonation promulgates missed signals, bonkers reptilian approbation who girdle with succeeding clunk. My's the arrangement interlock out of fecund peel, root beer hiccup on breath mint allowance. Particle epistle physics: persnickety Gargantua. Inordinate paroxysms of flux to weave the swatch. Which makes which please the iodides garrulously stain.

Waiting for a something that when it arrives changes nothing. Connotation of cluster, impediment, ocean of veils. Remarkable window fan who forced to pertain wishes clear plastic rope.

Immolate, inculcate.

Quixotic destitution on spun team jettison—*in carbolic delicto* simpers as winched fuselage carves enticement out of liquified masonry. Body shucked over garbanzo brain default (succotash canoe piperest oarsman set). All that belongs to, of incorporating, is and is to itself, without robbing of its. We are, perhaps to say, premature with afflatus.

The Last Puritan

The view was nothing to him

~

He would have been bored to run about
simply by himself

~

Personality began to percolate, as
it were, into his own

~

If a pebble got into his
shoe, it might be unpleasant

~

be stoically climed

~

he felt it again in a
different place

~

even if the wealth of nature,
but he took all this fervid
instruction a little more sullenly,

had to be pointed to, described,
thought of at such a moment,
or invent grounds of sympathy

～

old perambulator

～

Pebbles insignificant
accidents, like certain needs
of the body

～

but as to frills

～

sphere, was, as it, made, of,
perfectly, (glass

～

his bent, when he sat in, & beat
time to measure

～

anything merely seen or heard

～

have grown out of, & mixture,
was an original (though he
wasn't taught to *pray* them)
& even to sing a little
german songs

∾

these lasts were his favorite
amusements

∾

this was a great thought

∾

or heard remained a picture

∾

once moralized, the orange
squeezed

∾

deflated pulp

∾

in German, as well as in
English, or better

∾

& of course it would be
very wrong

~

inadequate to frame an
answer

~

merely held

~

It was a vast relief to
find himself in most
of the action

~

well out in the open

~

A great lunatic asylum
at his door, but he had
never visited it

~

but here was—— again
in person

~

Pride to seem, began, insufficient,
unnecessary

≈

his bare legs

≈

in spite of strange webs

≈

on deck, already sextant, because
wider, more unkempt, &
"being in business" had
no idea that so young
a fellow could be as
old as that

≈

"But I *am* bored."

≈

as disappeared to
work out his observations

≈

His views might be wrong,
but at least he had his wits
about him

~

but there, too, everything
made a rumble in his
head

~

But Walt Whitman is as
superficial as Rousseau

~

home wonderfully

~

goggles seemed

~

a thin old man at the
tiller

~

"Gad, we're clever"

~

He is over a hunchback &
built a Benedictine monastery,
I used to climb as a boy,
an enthusiast who has gone

over to Salem in his old
family orchard

～

with woeful results to
my digestion

～

These were his moments
intuition

～

he seemed to know where
everything was

～

hands more quickly than
ice

～　～　～　～

Acquiescence

A man comes into my
truck and criticizes my horse.
The ghost of a regret
dazzles its disrepair. Lions shape
mottled accents on descending temper.
Environs invoke the southern approach.

Approach environs my horse. Southern regret
criticizes a man. The ghost temper
the dazzles. Descending accents mottled shape.

The invoke dazzles ghost
into shape. Regret lions
its disrepair. Mottled environs
approach descending regret. A
horse criticizes the southern
accents on a temper.

Disrepair mottled my
ghost. Horse shape
accents on descending

disrepair invoke man.

Lions southern environs.

Truck dazzles approach

temper its regret.

Foreign Body Sensation

Such hills as hive me waste away

in the refulgent concatenations of failed

display. Most marvelous

of all, contraptions

the hand, of mind, makes pace

in sensory profusion

to trace the gates. Entering more

slowly than auction might allow, a brim

of distal craves avenue to mutter

on. The clutter

of this solemnity induces

for a pretense what hearers mask

anew. Sarcastic

chirps, refined alarm, will favor

for its suasion darts and

balm. Aviators

know the price of calm.

Yet land-locked coteries

defer from what

they want, unmitigated

handouts, unerring

bumps. Toys

to hunger for

a hankering, systematic

seals of aquamarine,

sleds portrayed (weighlayed)

against whose barn?

So there becomes a boating solid

retained quite anappropriately 2 points

off true Mercury. The of token

as intended, remanded to a building

block subtended, cowering

in grass of glass (the

meadow of the undivided

dividend) or yokes its yank

to curvilinear harbinger.

Her in played other the while

him into herself thrust & opened

his spread. Himself as other

the & around turned later.

The unfamiliar necessities of familiar

places. "But I do feel myself bumping . . ."

Three-quarters of a dozen of us
massed — hideous sentence. Camptown
Races, colithiasis cases.

"Why do you say that?"
"Because it annoys you."

A heart as big
as a sewer and a
brain as big as—
but comparisons
are innocuous &
the first lie
replicates itself
in an isolated
word. *Judge*
less you not
be judged
& the world slip
by unknown
you to it
it to you.

"I come here & I see

all these people from my hometown

give me a warm welcome. It

make me feel good, it give

me strength."

AN IMPORTANT NOTICE ABOUT YOUR RATES

You put your whole self in

You put your whole self out

You put your whole self in

& shake it all about

move to later

The spire of this

irrevocable rending

wets the path

just enough for

the treachery of

a slant glimmer.

Syncopation against

the borderline.

"Forget the blue. Nobody's
ever advocated blue."

"She could've been
the champion, but she wasn't
exposed to the right opponents,
no one who would extend
her."

Charmed
by his own regard

death is the Pall
that skewers All

"I am especially interested in the treatment of depression. With my
Lord and Savior Jesus Christ at the center of my life, I have found
real Joy and Purpose in dedicating myself to the Truth of His
Teaching as Written in the Bible. What gives the job it's excitement
is working with Stan Richards, a nationally recognized creative
wizard: *Adweek* recently named our agency among the eight most
creative in the U. S. I moved into this area after six years in the
aerospace industry, which I entered after early retirement from a
career as a venture capitalist and real estate developer. This has
been a stimulating opportunity for my work on late Pleistocene
and early Holocene environmental changes. Pat is currently in Sri
Lanka helping organize sera collection for leprosy patients.
Nowadays, being a husband, father, homeowner, and Jew keeps me
both busy and satisfied. I find myself immersed in a foreign but

also satisfyingly tangible world of container shipping. I still find the labor movement to be the (imperfect) representative of worker's interests, and the necessary base from which the realization of class structure in economic and social life are explained and organized into coherent, worker-oriented politics. It wasn't long before I found myself in the company of a spiritual adept who teaches the most profound way of transcendence of every kind of self-possession. Left the firm and freelanced in stained glass. I studied hula seriously in Hawaii and taught Hawaiian dance locally, forming a group to hire out for bar mitzvahs and luaus. To my knowledge this is a unique occurrence, of great spiritual and cultural significance. My work has taken me into the area of robotics and industrial automation. For several years I worked in insurance, specializing in kidnap and expropriation coverage. A professional interest has been in the area of domestic violence; I love the work and feel strongly about violent crime. For a while, I served in the Peace Corps in Guatemala as a nurse working with cancer patients. After two years in Met State, I became increasingly eager to work with severely disturbed children. I am beginning to dabble in writing screenplays, humor, and poetry. What time is left I devote to coursework at the Divinity School, where I am studying for the priesthood. It seems I have done other things also, but maybe not. I guess I. In the future, I look forward to the private practice of pathology. Just when that will occur is uncertain. I am now administering substances to others to alter or obliterate their consciousness. The break is wonderful. Though nothing has educated me as well as watching my father walk the picket line in a strike that was eventually broken."

was then on top of

without the benefit of elegance

almost in

over into transparency

I rode all night

my wetness fogging the path

Team Bias

Fun, you got
a funny way
of taking the
tail by the
horse. Around
who I glimmer
to stammer, rest
my eyelids on
an organized
social disclosure —
fine to meet
the heat on
the street.

Searchless Warrant

Germinal detonation inculcates missing resemblance

not otherwise pared, or, wishing you'd said, sank

curtly, brusque insolence narrowing on dated theatrics,

brutalized homilies to regulated mists. The parson

takes the moment to wish for a speedy return in a gabardine

suit. Drips decorate the porcelain, view

is emblazoned on polished pretense, insular

monuments. A restive restraint corrals

the aroma; reception areas are cordoned

off in other words liquid laminated. Restraint

takes a breather, ripping through halls of necrotic

prostration, autochthonous

titillation. Vehement interlocution denudes reptilian

cleavage (fiduciary squirrels). The allot is haggle

ecstasy, spec'd out on charm. Embue is given but

shifty (mobilized wingspan). She detours at torn

shock. Brays beguile injection, reduplication

of absolves, if invincible

lobby fever, nest on the town: vindicates aviation. Eyes

tumble (encaged encaustic). Who emblem ablative decoration,

marsh keyed at vagrant tusk. The or angiotropic

miasma (charisma): sputter at ooze. Gulled by splash,

guttered by inadvertent remission. Then unbutton

your presentient irritation, take coil for

describe, which powers moody harbingers. These ammo planes

blast all semblance of decorum—jaded lids

of betterment's employ. Search or set upon, entitling

harbors. For instance, detonate when you mean debutante,

fan when furnace. Stalk of at what within which lords:

neuter shibboleth. For instance, vaccination when you indicate

stormwindow (saronged widow). Increments of routine

disinterest disabling trapezoids: trampolines of the

spleen.

Amblyopia

He was a moral dwarf in a body as

solid as ice. Everywhere he looked

he felt fear and

evasion. No notice

no location bore any

resemblance to the true

form of these cinders:

intransigence, pestering. It

was the logic of

insurgence, a stone door

opening onto a dirt

floor. For three weeks

he stayed there, only 50

feet from the geyser

watching his footsteps

rattle. From time to

time, he rolled up the floor

and looked to the expanse

below. The physical

present, he would say

to himself, is unrelated to the

physical afterthought. Towns

steamed in the

light: a glimmer

of the ghosts of the people who had

lived there.

Personality is barbarity

so we eat at each other

with waxing spirits when

all the time we are on the

wane. No stop exists

except what we manufacture

the need for. The Heart

is a steel brace that men

use to erect their sagging spirits.

I am not I because my

sister has stolen a

pear and I have tasted of

its pit. The light

was (is) stuck. Mourners gnaw

at the columns.

Allegorical micturition has swept

the guest halls of the art galleries

and the undermasses

wail in the background to iambic

beat. Sludge is proclaimed sludge,

hairdos hors d'oeuvres, as the soiled

face of inverted cardioerasty—a.k.a

genital fetish—rears its mushy brow.

The excellence of our gifts humbles

us into cleverness when before we were

only foolish. *Blessed are the grieved* for

they at least have seen their

inheritance; the rest wait in maxivans

to collect as available. THE BITTER COKE

OF JIMMY CARTER; the greased palm, the

adored swan; all are crepuscular,

dilated, dogged, dictated. For others,

orgasm is achieved only by means

of words without any tactile contact;

some married women report depraved

husbands who force them to submit

to this practice. "It may be cheap

but it's not worth that much."

From the Ministry of Psychological Science:

Normal minds never run adrift when there are no environmental
factors to poison them. Exposure to big businessmen, right-to-life

Christians, military officers, career managers, and *New York Times* cultural editors causes otherwise healthy young people to become perverts. These types, motivated by greed for money and power and authority belong to the lower human strata. They are classed as moral imbeciles. They are all, or most of them, antisocials with a pronounced defective aesthetic sense. It is not uncommon, however, to find them brilliant and nimble witted. But they are plausible and ready liars. They lie even when the truth might be more serviceable. Lifestyles that would arouse horror and repugnance in normal persons are sought after by such individuals. People of this type resent being spoken to courteously; they want to be addressed roughly. Even among those classed as intelligent, they derive actual gratification in exposing their ignorance to one another. Many have anesthetic consciences—pricks with needles cause no pain. Orgasms can only be achieved by this type of pervert by enacting or fantasizing racist, sexist, ageist, or authoritarian acts. Having once been an unwilling witness to conversation between two such individuals, I can say it is the most disgusting, absolutely the most nauseating, spectacle one can imagine.

Solitude and contentment are the product

of the mystical; we are never

alone and, by rights, never at peace.

Such is a space that, called

into being, or given,

transforms everything from what we

know it to be, mishandled by

the world, to what it never was, blessed.

(Or handled: but since there is

no correct way to handle, it amounts

continuously to the same.) A bed of

smoke and pearls—tripped by

the sum, troped by the tune. No

cordon ever warms the soul, but

a simple costless gesture may. Yet

the act is not made but found, nor

yet discovered—nothing hides.

So begins the long march to the

next world. Custom is abandoned

outright as a criterion of moral

conduct. Everything must be justified

before the courts of the New Criteria, which

spring out of the old with the resourcefulness

and tenacity of the truly ingrained. The theory

of primary colors is rejected as elitist

empiricism and the wavelengths of the spectrum

take their proper and equal place in

the constitution of perception. Garrulousness

is taken for honesty.

Related to this—the excitement, the dancing

around, articulating itself in terms of these,

& getting, this might, the sanctioned

"drive and concentration", more

obviously through—dinner, TV—

in some sense entertained ("I tried

all kinds of things")—"open

ended" "divergent level"—as to

rehearsal, to assume the spirit of,

balanced against, practically

speaking, an unresolvable fend.

As harmful regardless, at which

at in was assessment, without

circumstance to enter, to be found in,

& often strategic almost total compensation,

hallmark comparably, innately

literally, operate by, overstatement,

endorsement, restriction, as if it

was already having our, as the

most, she or he along, suspect

that, that which, putting aside,

as such, cadres of the (steaming,

identification, insofar) in which

segmenting, say to stay,

technologically gathered, etc.,

into mass utter anomaly with,

if you hold, "get ahead" hot

bed, fosters as being outside

one is "alertness" or for

tapped, assigned, passed over,

inverted. A highly visible necessary,

& those is a safety valve to as

usual, designated but saved from the

meantime, would present, there is also,

apart from these, regarding are

largely.

The tubs rectify obliquely whatever

they decant, but this is not a

guarantee of much more than ingestion.

Whether there is a forge or a

spill, such that what is

represented is regarded with

spears, or does alarm come along

like, what's the vision and what

the version, a bland potentate

of flak. These are

ordinary triads. Why not recover

the innuendo of stultification

the grey gloat of glory?

For instance, hopping a pail, chewing

a nail, while all along a bone

spoke in the crag. Gushes of

static cling. It is not the eye

but it's gleam of which we dream.

This is my suffice to a world of

toast, "which so raptures the

spirits, delights the gust, and gives

such airs to the countenance as are

not to be imagined by those who

have not tried it". Apostate

rings girded by avalanche.

Whose history demands

carbon, which insinuate

formaldehyde. Discipline demands

not looking back, depotentiate dirigible

doorjambs, districted lapilli

thus extended: sworn fuss, brazen

discretion.

Shuns (shuts) tourmaline—indigestion

apparently apocrypha, red line.

Beeline to inadequacy, repossess pose

(by posse?) Integration of burn at distal

curve: go, gum, go. Govern get

away, resettlement crematoria, dog's

duty, prioritate. What's in it for (John's

Hancock)? Oblique cartel, gummed up

gust. Free clogging restored, myst-

ified. The harmony of harangue (dodeca

do(dad, mom)). With all the passion of

a plum, bowl of milk. Ha! see end

of (adobe).

INFORMATION ABOUT THE RATE ON PURCHASE

AND THE BALANCE

BY WHICH EACH IS JUDGED. The

Balance of every Purchase is an average

Daily Balance. Each daily Purchase

is added in the Life Cycle for, as

applicable, Purchase incurred before

the Conversion Date and Purchase incurred

on or after the Conversion Date. Each

day is begun with the opening Balance

for the Life Cycle for whatever Purchase

and all new Purchase and other

debts are added (including any posted

that day), subtracting all Payment and other

Credits posted to the Principal since the start

of the Life Cycle (including any posted

that day). The Daily Balance for Purchase

incurred on or after the Conversion Date

is as follows: each day is

begun with the opening Balance for the

Life Cycle for Purchase and all New Purchase

and other debts posted to the Principal

since the start of the Life Cycle (including

any posted that day), subtracting as before

(including any posted that day). However

there is no Balance for

Purchase incurred either before or on

or after the Conversion Date in any

Life Cycle in which there is no

Previous Balance for Purchase, or in which all

Payments and other Credits applied to Purchase

for the Life Cycle at least equal the

Previous Balance for all Purchase for the

Life Cycle.

Thus will these hovers goad, the lurk's

amount to saddle its detour, relinquishing

two snares and a brandy-colored

drain, inside themselves, and six

pace on, to halt at precipice. No

peace abjures like the bleat of desalinated

tears, with which to wash tomorrow's

coarse inveigh. Consider stance a

suck upon portent's languid sneer.

The world grows simpler, or I

ajangle in its pores—so

simple one might dote upon

refrains or balk at balm.

"No other vision exists except

the single crane—they call it

tracking—on a green-brown

backing."

Neither for what or without—

An incredible growling hush besets, or

sets over, this pall of purpose. Testing

the certitude of fortitude, the quiescence

of restitution. Everything as it always

was, or will (would) want to be—

ferreting a cataract from a sublime

act, the knees and pancreas of boisterous

dispose. Mildness and omitted

emotions.

Everything external to turn

of the last out of accumulated, dig

slowly, piles trying about, which were

flaw, fugitive, indeed lights, but when

mind of stumbles that on accurate

has to do which became early, say

at, might just as it is, clash, that

by mainly intentions, subjected

as if, were—officious tone—nickel &

dimed or being any given to do

something that that on our—you

should, that is, to handle—even

come up with what amounts to, for

keeping or setting of respect of lack

literally trying to prolong, complain

apparent, is to rather condescended

correlative as to blind, off, by

attitude.

substitution dubbed

The clothes are clogged, the

blistering revamped, all the pleonasms

gone away. What chord, cowed

lingers as the lurker takes its

nightly flight? Beyond these realms—

ingots made of air; or not-quite

air, that less were substance of a dream.

Or beam remote into exaction

obliterated grace of stubborn hand.

Or in which ornate matter is dispersed

to the sarcophagi of circumstance

or in which, lamented by the swell

torches cascade in fractions of

notions left as

elevated or whether who so may, withstanding

lock, block, & pork—indiscriminate

originarys, reputable gulls, while

wistfully wandering at the end-platform

vouchsafing their—eye will already

spatter in dejectable detonate, re-

furbishment to high cantorial yarn

per yard would be cantankerously

mortuary, which fails, hales—

The new begins again, slips behind—

not more to wish than to redress,

sacrament of superfluity in the (a) realm

of frowns. There is a crimson

counter, an alabaster fountain—on

the other side.

Where do you want to ride? It's

all a matter of dejection & sub-

limation, illusion & collusion.

So called surreal surcease, badger

endeavour to enjoin. Here are heroes, bison

with functioning mindsets, dictaphone

artists, domestic doodlers. The cup-

cake of tranquillity, the earache of—

There is neither matter nor form, only

smell, taste, bite—eyes

hide by their disclosure. There

is only substance—structure—twin

fears of an unduplicating repetition:

the sandstorm of grief, the presentlessness

of distribution. As farfetched

ministers to its own resolve

purpose alone is the proprietor

of the poignant, vesture of solace's

lazy haze.

Keep a curb on your brain. The heart

beats thrice where the soul has lost

its foot. The campground of larceny

is the foremast of destination's deprecation.

Still, no teleology holds here. Gather

what rims you may, hold tight to

clandestine animation, besalt aggravation.

Out of a pure sludge . . . and to sludge
shall you—remain.

The heir of circumstance, the in of
inarticulation. Stepping off a
train, a station liner, a moth
ball. Floating into incandescent frostbite.
How these avenues arise in arrears.
Joining our Savior, boring our way
here. I've got—why not get—
strip cash, milk of

"He's made an art of not remembering."

The pierced fluidity of a smile that
battles reportorial mink stoles, solvent
greasers in gumptious dodecahedrons.
Why wet these belts, revamp
a tire? Milkmaid of respect, jilted
of dismay. Go, get, gone—

"Perception does not merely serve
to confirm preexisting assumptions, but

to provide orgasms with new
information." Standing around the
kitchen, talking 'bout boats.

A tool of philosophy.

Who (which) garner anyway, any-
where (why). Panes fly dirigibles, or
foment surface shimmer (chimera). Beige
lofts the two of us (whether) signalling
retreat—enhance—repeat—entrance. Slow
beat the bugles on Murray's soured
block—clappity clap, jiffity jig. There
is no refusal that outlives
handprints, suction weight. Thence
thwart a (of) formica biscuit cut-
ter, all through the seas. A clue 'ugs
butter—(vats)—

Many people have trouble with everyday
activities, such as speaking, thinking,
responding, dreaming, eating, sleeping. A crutch
shares the weight of burden, protecting

without shielding, but should not be used
without specific instructions.

Untoward by—these detach with
salmon or scrubmate severance
not anywhere detained by
oaken chair, wavering as the wind
whirls around Brenda Starr, eschatological
venison. I abide by later
egging, tomahawk remonstration.
Or is this gulled, posted, and
foreshortened? Who activates
you biscuit us insets, um,
er, insects. Colonies of spears,
a minority of heres.

cares caned

Whoever therefore blemishes into
interlock—defamed retainer, absorbent
factotum. Which wish reserves
armoire. Here he lunges (interpeptide
nudge) at workmanlike manure, sharp

presser. Ache of the pancreas, fate
of the polyurethaned didact. Emblemized
by tries.

The flip side of organdy—still
lace face, fretted surprise, "Jam"
Whistler. An or am emendation of
beside all preemptive repair. Gliding
in indigo boxcars, hiding in
viewmaster canister. Golan Heights
swollen price.

No scheme completes the falling down
of chairs, of cards, or igloos
sprayed in camel dust. The motion
spares the inbred count, where
clumps at curious coventry steam
seas of sailors' sorrows.

From this adoration unrolls more smoke—
eyed voyeurs with whooping
coughs. Those afterward, strolling
out of their lofts and heliotropes

displacing memorized variety

with hallucinogenic contempt, lather

up their secretions and spew them

at— Convicted of charm

conspicuous with greed.

And Now . . .

Texton introduces the Whipmaster Valorizer™

Yes . . .

Just when you thought you were stuck in the same

old shopworn anxieties and tired-out guilt

feelings, the Whipmaster Valorizer™ has arrived,

revolutionizing the psychopoetics industry.

In just seconds, you can turn your sordid dreams

and ambitions into cherished *res intellectiones*.

The Valorizer uses a unique Twofold action.

Negative associations are effaced from habitual

cognitions by a sanitized derealization process.

Simultaneously, positive associations are affixed

to these cognitions by means of thousands of tiny

Idealization Crystals®, a unique adhesion agent.

The Whipmaster Valorize™ is available exclusively

from Texton, your better living through alchemistry
company.

"What is this, a marathon?" Strolling in
admonition, bowling in derivation. Weave our
way in mordant display. For a day
is not a dome, nor an estuary a
delegation. Reminiscent of restitution, perennial
towel-master, tuck-a-way bonfire, cloaks
the longing for lard (largesse). Museum of
double blinds: clubbable behind, whereless weathers.

Locations lock the far side of.
Not that riddles, little by little a
momento of seed; oasis of reproach
gusts the beatitudes tiny stare, lording
it over sword sway. Imperial
allure at ground zero. Forget,
forfeit. The journey is stern
benefactor to the departing caboose.
Ride the querulous hound.

Total Body Clearance

The order of immaculate nomenclature

casts a paled glance at what,

fearful in its haze, regales with

trenchant ease. In craters

bound for hideout in determine,

elevate a gift for pleats to

Gordean possession of a disappearing

knot. Food changes what is

hitherto unmentioned—juggled

prisms in a boot of clay.

Perfume spills so odor might

yet linger, the cringing charm

outweighs the portal's breach.

Prosthesis

The foreman's salt ambassadors my liveried state: yes I
Among the photometric isolates reeve without kind or
Kilter, a boat of purely ruddered, awake upon a sea of
Sand. You give me mote, some blame to spike,
While gracious ghosts repair to fall; not sloping
Pods or pelted pumps, display is will's entrapment
To the tune of thud red bows. Coordinate in time to
Tassel, kangaroo pears and blushless perk, or semiseek
The way to curl a quarrelsome blouse, a thirsting pan:
By dint admixed to churn's inveigh. So
Frail at slide would tend a grin into a
Lobster's pocket, chirps of surfeit in a potato's eye.
The larger ambush forked, the truer stung
To glint, attached with peering ram into
The scene of love's dejection, rust's delay. No
Firm inversion set upon bent tools: caves of
Straw in fields of gold. Function sets adrift the
Tone of squander—crease today for tomorrow we may
Ply. A bobbing pride, a sequenced dereliction—
Cooly tarring the advent of embark. At any
Moment, send up, swirl, inquire septum, throttle
On: invisible
As disappearing ink, a residue haunts the quietest nights.
"Forged of life itself
Lofty ideas, heroic deeds,
Accomplished in the name of the Final Triumph."
All ears, no tears. The earliest
Bridge of solid yoke—take spears to prove
A gambit, fleece a brag, what
Echo makes of mooning. Dead
Pleats in a detonated garage. Tresseling
Tinderboxes, sleep inflicted yammies with buzz along
Fan belts. These guys gets my gulp. Absolute silence,
Bordered by Magdalenian equipoise. All skin and
Bones and no place to hide. Monotony is bliss,
So said the Matterhorn to Edward Whymper.

Use No Flukes

Close to stand

Glitter with edge

Clouds, what's, but

Weather of devoid

Uses unwrapping

Lower the second

Gravity for allowing, but

Slowly, as if

Backward, falling

Folded

Safe Methods of Business

The Sleepy impertinence of winsome actuarials
Lambs me to accrue mixed beltings—or,
Surreptitiously apodictic, impedes erstwhile.
Pumice, for instance, has bowdlerized the steam
As amulets of oddments cedar coatfins
Or rake about shoals. The pig is stabbed
Through the belly (horse grippings are not essences).
For choice is rivulets. The chase of
Carolinas cries in the gorge—not so
Much ranting as astringent. And therefore
I have mailed the teas and come, an
Old man with a wet mouth, when invited.

"They're starting to start up the cranes." & so
For a long while Sophia bade her time
A sorrowful adieu and sat in un-
resplendent edginess near the wharves' waves.

Where are the blue sputter of
yesteryear? "Sometimes
I think I hear
a mosquito but it turns out to be the
Refrigerator." "It's not so
bad once you get used
to it." Always keeping
the Ball on the proverbial
Eye. Can't
be afraid and can't
not to. The
Fear that made Milwaukee
fake it. "I
told the man I would
jerk sodas
for him at his counter
But

I would never prostitute
myself for that fee." Having
captured the two Frankish princes, Balak
marched on Aleppo, seized
it from his cousin
Suleiman despite
frenzied resistance by the
populace and
then, like his
uncle Ilghazi four years
earlier, set out
To invade the principality of Antiod. "I
don't think you should give
choice to a nine-
year-old. A thirteen-
year-old maybe." It's
Hard to be fair
and just at
the same
time. For instance,
according to *Boston*
magazine, Oliver Wendell
Holmes once
called the city "the hub
of the solar system".
"Fire!"
"That is enough, I
won't bring you again!"
Why Women Admire Liberace.

The dead, dull hours of summer's interminable days
On which no hope, nor shadow, sets to
Bring surcease of this blanched wildness.

Putting her proverbial Toe in the waters, her
Temptors. Narcotic of little care: wailing against
A wall, braiding a gall. The tree has lost
Its neon and beams in sacerdotal douchings
Of incontinent magisterium. Nor changed
Transformed into a seeing
Barred by trial—but released to it, in
It. Several indissoluble esplanades
Less arbitrary than lived in. The
Flesh, smeared as ersatz materiality, among
Whom we multiply. Long dormant the better
To well over—less metonymic than
Inimitable. Forsake the bow, embrace the
Churl. Which braves
It to either destitution, just off
Right of Constitution Caverns.

CAUTION: MARINERS ARE WARNED TO STAY CLEAR OF THE
PROTECTIVE RIPRAP SURROUNDING NAVIGATIONAL LIGHT
STRUCTURES.

No rest for the wicked, less for the pure in heart.
Teetering at pause in regulus, masthead of rig &
Splay—ablative command in dative array. Peculiar
Pester pursuant to penury. Nor thought at.

"That's the way he called it, caught it." Bituminous
Wings ablast bullocks—pummel of inter-
Tracing, or drains panes. Here so beset upon,
Becalms.

Everybody wants to be a philosopher—serrated
Or otherwise. As for instance as cream as
Perpetuates as in lacquer or lacrity ransoms
Asymptotic dissuasions as freedom's necessity,

Necessity's freedom. Jump or jumble
(Crumble). The boar symbolizes the Ox while
Near dissects instinct. Rather than post-
Ponement what we have is a premature
Arriving but with unlimited potential for further
Arrivings which, translated to the sexual, gives
Rise to theorems of delay. You can swim
Or you can float—there's no metaphysical
Difference; yet history is *made*.

The tide is red (just another Jewish American
Peasant) and the beanstalk
Broods—a rocker for Syncopation
Day. I mean filtration not sediment
(Sentiment)—bumps you stash with
Angelic piquance. Blotter when
Blobbed (the origin of *écriture* [scribbage]).

The summons charges me with parking at a crosswalk on the
northeast corner of 82nd street and Broadway on the evening of
August 17, 1984. The space in question is
east of the crosswalk on 82nd street as indicated
by the yellow lines painted across the street. This space
has been a legal parking space during the over ten years I
have lived on the block. Cars are always parked in this space
and have continued to (unticketed in several observations I
made yesterday and today). Apparently, new crosswalk markings
are currently being painted in white on both 82d street and
83d street. At this time, the process is not complete.
When these new lines are finished, several spaces may be
eliminated. However, as they looked at the time I received
the ticket, they did not appear to override the yellow lines
according to which I was clearly in my right to park in the space.
If there is a change being made in the regulations, it seems
unfair to penalize before new lines are clearly imprinted.

I am sure a check of traffic department activities will show
this work in process rather than complete at the time of the
ticketing. I parked without any knowledge that regulations were
changing, conforming to practices legal over the past decade.
As a resident of the block, I feel there should be adequate notice
that parking regulations are being changed—if in fact they are—
and that it is unjust to ticket before new indications are
fully in place and while the preceding yellow lines are
left intact.

"If you've got a wayward 17-year-old, it's
going to be tough getting him or her to give you
a urine specimen," concedes Mr. Reuter, who
has tested his own five children. "But then,
if they won't give it to you, you know
you've got a problem."

"Officials in Washington believe confidence
can't be restored as long as a daredevil
is in the pilot's seat. 'It isn't just a move
to get Charlie out. It's a major motion.'"

LINT
There are trains and there is pain
As when a signet skips, a gurgle sighs
You tender chance, employ a tug
Sooner than equation, furthered by
An ounce of quell: despondent cheer or
Netherworldly plug who sprain
Of factious things, trebled and
Makes halls, most noisy knit that
Jaws it chewed, slump clearance
Toward anon

Lines are like that—you stop, sort
and then you waiver. *You?* I only
mean to hobble along to the meeting
and save some ground until then.
The mind is a dam all right, costs
a lot of God damn taxpayer money to
keep it from leaking. The mine is
damned all right, lost a ton of, &c.

I am charged with parking in a no parking anytime zone
restricted for U.S. Mail. I did park on West 35th street just
west of Seventh Avenue about 3:45 on
Sunday afternoon (9/2/84). The only parking sign
visible indicated that parking regulations for this section of
the street were not then in effect. There was no yellow line
nor any trace of postal activity or a post office building.
Subsequent to being ticketed, a
search of the area indicated that considerably
up the street but obscured from the space I parked in
was a sign attached to a building exterior—that is this
sign was not adjacent to the curb, where NYC parking notice
signs are customarily placed, but lying against the building on the
inner side of the sidewalk. Because this sign was
not posted at curbside and was out-of-view, it was inadequate
to give notice that the curbside sign was to be superceded
especially since there was a clearly visible curbside sign
in the usual place, which univocally stated that parking
restrictions were not in effect on Sundays. I ask
that this ticket be dismissed.

A kind of state of

subaltern lunacy

armed or expressed

to about the

sum of say

Loquacious Motors

whence, by device

stronger 'en gourds

pretending to be

pony rides, I'll

alter not depend

the mailtruck

as when

harpsichord jangles

over the eaves

looked out, er, locked out

sin helo

ripp(l)ing off into

buttoned-up

boostercables.

MORAL VIEW
Inconceivable in fact that waves
                                in such
        proportion, that
become a
    weathering.
                                do
but   to   spume

of
   seascape   and a freezing spoon
   nearly full, but risen
      proper place at
      quite
          and gulls
    back, it is the
       most, enclosed
glowering like
         a fault, the cold
       combine
    of things,
  various
     sometimes
        does,

And so we returned to our basic question—
How in heaven do you get an outside line?

Errors have a way

of clawing in the blight

like pawns or ponies

to their anointed

spheres, so coiled

in stumping, or

impress of

clamps, these

halls & barriers

who reprove &

grasp, an arc

of meshed perturbs

and head-first, on it

lopes afloat the

spoil, having

carried or careened

to pumps

& clumps.

One wants to be a stranger but retreats
into familiarity, into the face of a
coin, a spearhead nickel. Bounding by
two frames, a concept unhinged in
its quiescent sag or sap, of whom
is better to say "no glup, no
pedimento". Too many crooks spoil
the sidewalker, at least up to and
excluding, four-and-one-eighth,
$22.95. Merely myopic, queerly
entokened, . . . the only true boats the ones
that have never sailed, nor been wet
by these kept oceans.

Why I Am Not a Christian

One holds these promises (holds
to them) amidst the make-believe
mayhem of another day
each farther from
that resolution in renouncing
aspired to as cat its
pawn. You always throw it down
but you never pick it up. Everything
everywhere circumscribed by its
physical, which is to say habitual
array, the necessity to order what
is otherwise always possible. The frequent
opportunities I have possessed of
observing the thousand acts of amiability
and kindness, feeling by conduct turned
to expectation and ripened to
remorse. You cannot suppose
and cannot not to. The
freight is slumberous friend
to a commoded journey—nearly
a smile or only a poor
bred thing. Profits will
never displace the value of
this self-made masquerade.

A Person Is Not an Entity Symbolic but the Divine Incarnate

1. *The Behavioral Despair Model*

Rats are placed in gallon beakers of
water for fifteen minutes. After several minutes they
stop struggling to escape and assume an
immobile posture. This swim is to condition
"helplessness". When placed in the beaker the next
day for a five-minute swim, the rats
don't even struggle for a minute, resuming
the immobile stance for the remainder of the time.
However, when drugged with an antidepressant
the rats' futile production
increases to over four of the five minutes
of the swim.

2. *Spring Shade*

Easy done it.
The flesh. Think of the last end
Intoxicate, & the flosses of the sty:
Leaves, showering
Falling on wool, or clouds of thought
Conditioning terms & times.
They say: "This driving thing
Two stilts already
Far out, rising & crawling
Fine spooks glittering. Clop clop.
& the velvet light on the lawns
Luminous, smug in the night
Eastward and weightless, grip by grip
All turns of grace
Posing, ignoble, noisy.
Trash blows in this congress. One by one.

3.

Just now back, one of the more on-the-edge
at plush, including one got-a-hold-of
definitely all these types, or something, but
then and anyway saying that was of a kind
of condition (old dilemma) is being pulled
in front of the obvious. Right now am
is the only obvious (what with the cold, snow, rain)
and just trying to immerse so can get onto
other things. That probably explains: how do
you get out of a line of anecdote that starts
taking a direction you don't necessarily have
or want to express (expose?). I will
get back to your thoughts when I
have the time to think adequately
on them.

4.

"You're about as easygoing as a car skidding on ice."

5. *Clotilde, from Apollinaire*

Anemone and aquilegia
Have sprouted in the garden
Where dorms the melancholy
Between the amour and the disdain

It comes there also our umbras
Which the night disperses
The sun that rendered them somber
With them disappears

The deities of live water
Let flow their hair
Pass it's necessary that you pursue
This beautiful umbra that you want

6. *Personal Marketing Strategy*

"He's got a lot more talent than it takes to drive a cab."

7. *Latex Dummy*

I feel I mean I am I consider I can I wish I cut I find I wonder

I know I lie down I saw I dream I laugh out loud I experience

confusion I realize I slap my knee I feel closer I try I break

lines I shrug I answer I look I get at I lift I choose up

8. *The Value of Depression*

Between fifteen to twenty million Americans—two thirds of them
women—are medically diagnosed as "depressed". In 1982, thirty-one
million prescriptions were written for antidepressant drugs
generating over two-hundred-sixty-five million dollars
in sales. Elavil and its generic equivalent imipramine
and Tofranil and its equivalent amitriptyline still
account for most of the sales—but there is stiff
competition from a number of newer drugs since the
high profit potential lures the major drug companies
to develop and heavily promote new products. In
1981, two of the leading antidepressant manufacturers
spent four million dollars each on promoting their already
best-selling drugs—seventy percent of this money going to
"detail men" who sell the drug in face-to-face
meetings with psychiatrists, family doctors, and internists.
Two new drugs were backed up by promotional spending of
eight million dollars and thirteen million dollars each. In
addition to promoting the use of antidepressants
and the advantages of their particular brand, detail
men are also instructed, for instance, to convince
physicians to prescribe the "recommended" doses
of the drug instead of the common practice of prescribing

a one-half or two-thirds dose to moderate side effects.

Underdosing is seen as a major problem for the dollar

return of the product.

9. *Sonata for Unaccomplished Cello* by SUSAN BEE

rum	darps de ballet
paino	clute
boboe	woloist
celbo	flue
vice	conduster
basset	saxopone
boule bass	dymphony
cellop	flits
rumpet	viola da bamba
harpsichjord	composted
oopera	Engkish horn

10. *Parasol Parade*

I want it as much as anyone.
I am constantly made aware of how different I am.
They ask me, "Are you always so uncomfortable?"
They make you feel like they could care less.

It's not that I don't like them.
Sometimes I feel an attraction.

You're continuously nervous, you mumble, you stutter.
You say to yourself, "They can't possibly understand."

11.

12. *Literary Theory*

"There is a whole genre of geese in the tin toys."

13. [CHORUS:]

People should love and approve of me. Making mistakes is
terrible. People should be called on their wrongdoings. It's
horrible when things go wrong. I can't control my emotions.
Threatening situations keep me worried. Self-discipline is too
hard. The bad effects of my childhood still control my life.
I can't stand the way most people act: avoiding responsibility,
terribly unfair, always late, demanding attention, physically
abusive, putting things off, harshly critical, whiny
or crybaby, withdrawing into themselves for
days or weeks, drinking too much, smoking, sleeping all the
time or not at all, afraid of their own worthlessness,
angry, irritable, bored, dull and frustrated, lonely, paralyzed,
hopeless.

14.

that I could be on
& still in

or is it just coincidence
I make meaning of

complaining always
a picture of complaint

directions of energy
substance, a direction

or figment
that blinds

seen, fixed
but by this

summoning of contusions
sorted, grained

among constellations
of indifference

15.

                        is like a
                                is a
        its
                one has a conception
looks
        wants somehow
    stares at
                    that it
        some kind of
                        who is not
            allowing for
            that they be there
    everything one must
                        it's a very

16.

"Are you happy, *Jack*?"

17. *"Billions for Bandaids": The Individuation of Sickness*

None of the advances in internal medicine, surgery, or

the whole range of symptom-and-treatment medicine that were the

primary commitment of nineteenth century medicine had

even a tiny fragment of the positive impact of public

health measures (cleaning up the sewers, feeding the hungry)

that were the underfunded scorn of the medical establishment

and the governments that headed its priorities. The

valorization of the "internal man"—the construction of
the self is a construction of a personalized body as
much as a personalized mind—has taken its greatest toll
against the accreditation of the *social* body as the primary
site of human life and disease.

18.

*As we near the close of our High Holy Day services for
5745, in these last hours of the Day of Atonement, Yom
Kippur, let us say the litanies of confession,* oshamnu:

We are filled with guilt, we have been in
bad faith, we have transgressed
against others and we have mouthed
lies. We have tolerated evil and prodded
our hands to violence; we have been
presumptuous, broken trusts, caused hatred
and resentment, framed falsehood;
We have counselled in self-interest, we have
failed in promise, we have scoffed
the powerless, minded the powerful, and blasphemed
against hope; we have rebelled too
little against injustice, we have been
selfish and arrogant, we have oppressed;

We have done badly, we have

corrupted ourselves and committed abominations;

we have gone astray and have led astray;

We have turned aside from our collective

good and it has availed us not at all.

But you are right in

all that has become us,

you have acted truthfully

but we have wrought

despair. What shall we say

before you, who dwell

within, and what shall we

recount to you, who abide

in the heavenly and know

all things, hidden and

not hidden?

May it be our will to forgive and be

forgiven, may we grant, and be granted,

remission for all our transgressions.

19. Umbra, from Apollinaire

You there anew close to me
Souvenirs of my companions dead at the war
Olive of time
Souvenirs which make no more than one
Like a hundred furs make not than one coat
Like these thousand wounds make not than one article in the journal
Appearance impalpable and somber who have comprised
The form changing of my umbra
An Indian at the lookout during eternity
Umbra you crawl close to me
But you attend me no more
You will know no more the poems divine that I chant
Whereas me I attend you I see you once more
Destinies
Umbra multiple that the sun guards you
You who love me enough in order never to quit me
And who dance at the sun without making dust

      Umbra ink of the sun
      Text of my light
      Caisson of regret
      A god who humiliates himself

20. [*Michael Meeropol:*]

"You see it gets used, just as the case was used
in the fifties to create a monolith-
ic public opinion. You know, equat-
ing the Left with treason. So today . . . the same
old Red-baiting guilt-by-association
effort that succeeded so beautifully
in the 1950s. . . . That's the basic tact-
ic, it's always been divide and conquer. Ron-
nie Radosh would deny strenuously that
he's interested in playing divide and
conquer, and yet Ronnie Radosh wrote an art-
icle for *The New Republic* in which he
said the Communists ought to be kicked out of
the nuclear freeze movement to purify
it, to protect it. Well, this is just what the
Red-baiting liberals of the New York *Post*
said when they explained why they didn't defend
the First Amendment rights of Communists in
the 1950s. It's the same story all
over again. Once again, my parents are
held up as this example to be feared by
the liberals. They don't want to be tarred with
it. And the acceptance of the Radosh-Mil-
ton book by the Establishment is a per-
fect example of their effort to strike the
same kind of fear in the hearts of the left-lib-
erals as was struck in the 1950s."

21.

Perhaps have screened

Often all for

Furious as jump or frame

Thought that perplex so not would

Wait though shreds a thousand could

Outlast place staid or fold

Have made ends once

22. *To the Victors, the Spoiled*

There awaits a hallway of indelible
propulsion, adorned
with the tireless anticipation of
homing ground. Homeopathic
jostling only renders the point
mute: the scorn remains as blue
as its coterminous leavening. Or
taken by a gust, enclose
a veil as portent
of intolerant testimony to
the tribunal of greater despair
than you have ever known, or care
to.

23. *Edison's Bulb's Still Burning (or Writer's Block)*

"You're trying to take the sail out of my wind."

24. [FROM PAOL KEINEG]

Death maintains the verdure in his justness.
This is not the zone lyric with tufts of yellow and of
rouge—but the camp of stones dried and of fruit
burst.

On high, the mother of potatoes has blanched
cheeks—brilliant on the oats and chicory.

Blade enters the amoured, the nailed owl
to the nailed door. The tongue is gone for a
long time, but the mouth salivates.

Culpable not culpable for all manner of
all matter the babble of babel the debate of debuts.

25.

cuts so deep

upon layer & layer

fogs & clots

nothing

is adequate

against *ab*sense

26. *"Come, Shadow, Come"*

return to a shadow

as slope of mind,

veiled air,

(the way a thought will turn

with a gesture in its direction—

you are a thing

your voices are unreal

blade, pool,

paper, shavings

its glassiness waving for us

Rose the Click for 23

An' listen, okay, *key* central elbow sez crime's key tent arose infurious
Toot the night! yet encored the landman jay separate isolate lay
    choices tented dared or, duh, romp in vain, ill, ya
    to your blue bah, duh, rescue, duh, conductor's key
    person—nah—put, attend
Ooh, hun, relay inexplicable key *re* tablet lay sequences
Re end
Delay night—nigh due, landman, *re* end nest deconnectable
Elbow category cruel, lapped cruel, par trope cruel
    on nay sent extra Pa cess toot form keep rend
    legs is taunt
Ill, eh, Dan's the force delay—key vote
Rose jet dew, mound assorted ant Dan's liver
Rose tray different vassal key sashay
Crime-dew bow

Surface Reflectance

Your job, right at this moment, is to get busy on
the quality of your mental pictures. How, or
grabaway sideshow and rack, lamed under
pained glass with omniscient angle, runs a
rub-out of the hurdle, careening
to dunked mariachis. I thought, as I've
spent; the shrinking allegory of a pile of pent-
ecostal bromides, things no doubt overlapped for
indicative retention, of our in-the-nature mode—
things that but which strike more generally
in response of entertaining back. Completely
wide. Nor is there anything to answer, hence
the slowness is sufficiently primitive whereas
maybe do something like what claims clam
the most would liken as current as carried
over to dismiss: although no doubt arguments can
be made lankily open in isolation or anyway
solution, which of course explains
your interest in the implosive process, i.e. real
plates, is to the point trying to place. About whom
I know very little. When pretenses are introduced to each
other they shake hands standing; they may smile or at
least look pleasant. This is more apparent in

breaking without avoiding than can ever be

at the same timorous longing and mealymouthed

extirpation. In this way, naked

and closing, become

self-inflicted scars of a commitment to the

necessary but unwanted baby-with-the-tub-water dusk

mask. Not only because of but

doing and letting, however something

that requires dismal able and many since. Seems

like to be getting for being the rest of

but very much as contagious as hung

up. I'll

buy that but that beside the relative low-level

flailing just to say we have that despite

is quite sad. "Hundreds of thousands of years ago

our ancestors of the dim and distant past faced

these same problems." Nevertheless

the sun never lights the same

place twice. This is due to the fact that you

probably have never learned

emotional control. "Freezing

up and melting down: that's

the kind of token I am."

(Inflexible mastication, ingestible

renunciation.) Go get

bored (burrowed), the fuselage saturates for

the rest, the milk-toast prescience, preferred

spacebands. However, at this point, we shall introduce

screen prompts with character compensation. All

devices are on to the Controller and share the Controller's

intelligence. As a result, all components can operate

simultaneously so as to eliminate obsequiousness

and redundancy while lowering social costs, e.g.

plug-in—plug-out systems configured

to your exact aversions. "Boy, cut that thing

from under your waist and pull off

that jitterbug hat. You're on the chain

gang now." Belaboring a bumping

pride and orthostatic altercation: swashed

by procrustean maxiserve, the shrill is

exhumation. "So Tarzan of the Apes did the only

thing he knew to assure Jane Porter of her safety. He

removed his hunting knife from its sheath

and handed it to her." Even the most objectionable

people begin to seem benign once they take

an interest in you. I.e., "the stuff is on

now". Windbag winding around Seattle, the worse

for wetness. Now hit this

Studebaker sundeck, cottoning

megabacktrack. An irrepressible torque

meets an unsaturable torpor. . . . *on seas of*

brass, with knees of glass. Nor

introduce a woman to a man unless

he is head of state or head

of church. It's a quality I've always disliked, with a real

sense of acceptable (bar

certainly fell down if they strike you). Full sheaf of

which does justice and quite before making incredible

dullness and myopia, fly off or jump in generally

parochialism than if there was one, limited

attempt and hear allowing "thoroughly".

Misconstrues other more that come from having

seem of or more about them. Certainly glued

to what. Of course, I *do*; was inquiring, to the

extent of well am not convinced, oddly, on

completely covering-up. Scrupulous misrecognition.

Since one's relation to one's

is not to stand is both behind and ahead.

Not begin to, far from that. Here is

where we'd both. Even in as to what to have

and right also in the instance fairly patently

realize, have time to operate, no doubt

fuels. There can be. Even if some. Is

because it's. Felt finally contestable, cowardly

not to, which are probably at the bottom often

sourly missed. Yet echoes communicative compliance.

> And then we'll go axeroxing!
> Axeroxing! Axeroxing!

Now let's get back to the teenager whose emotional

life is not so exhilarating, the boy or girl who

goes to school, meets with friends an hour

or two afterward, possibly even helps around

the house later. The problem being

*under*nutrition not *mal*nutrition; personal choice

of 'healthstyle' is only the most marginal factor

in preventing disease. Candles are lit

and shades are drawn; the frappé

bowl is set up. "You ought

to see a doctor about those pains." "What

a bumper!" Ben looked at Debby. "That's

Daddy's name—his Hebrew name!" Taking

the blame, making it plain. The other images are tied

up in long-term deposit earning Heavenly interest for

the world to come between this and the next.

"Despite the disparaging

things that less fashion-alert males have said

about the chemise, Mr. Bernstein plans

to back it. He will risk

several thousand yards of material

which is what he has

set aside for this style. . . . Mr. Bernstein

has been known to sell as many as 12,000

copies of one style in the same week. . . . Of

course there are certain 'classics' that will continue

to sell and probably keep Mr. Bernstein

from closing up shop even

if he guesses wrong and cuts

thousands of dresses that buyers will never buy.

These classics include shirtwaist

dresses and full-skirted cotton with scooped

necklines." *And went down to the ship*

very bored. What has not been

made, what has not been

seen, what has not been

spoken: always in the folds of the

audible, visible

projection of desire: to launch

a care, munching a pear. *Mobile*

in the site, the piece is

pierced in sequence. Homily grits,

bungled pie. There is no

other, only recover. And then back down

to the ship very buoyed. Debby

had just about tied the bow of her pink

taffeta dress when she heard the porch

door creak open. "At least when I close

my eyes nobody can see me." Early

warning sighs. Buttressing broncho-

dilation, arcadian

microseconds jostling pansynchronic obsidian vases in the

collation of infrequent mention. As if

the only relief is to be from charitable

demagogues who give a hoot. Invaded by

sweat and reputation. Better blast

and run—can't hide *here*. For there's nothing

so much fun as overelaborating the

obvious. That is, "can't pin

you down" (evidently afraid

to be tied up). "I'll catch you

on the rebound." (Even the theoretical

balk is replaced by if they say.) The next twelve shouts

took a little bit more time: Enormous back up

at the bank. Silk worms or smoke

rings? *"You've got a beach bungalow*

where your brain should be!" "This nation

cannot endure half poor

and half garbage." There are many

things to say, much that can be truly said, but

little that needs saying. Acts

of meaning preempted as an absence

for want of repetition—the needing

is saying, the saying is meaning. Any you,

my friend, back away, & hear only dim

peals to dead throngs. I hear

them too, & you. Speak

to me so I may hear, speak

that I may speak. There are only

plain words, panes of our separation

and sameness in saying. Tell

me of another country and of

your blankest journeys, tell

of the colors you cannot contain.

Afraid of meaning, afraid

of the words, which are

its body.

          What do you got?
          Bubblewrap in
          Place of a heart?

"What a ceiling! What a ceiling!" So do

not ask for whom the phone rings—not likely

for you. I think it's time

we were all put to sleep. The

body, the

body. I, minimus of Amsterdam

shimmy on the waves, and torch

plunge and vanish. *Was*

Maurice Bishop killed because

he spoke English? WHOSE

Christmas? She doesn't dish it out

and she doesn't want to take

it. "I just bought it because

it came out." One day people will be judged

not only by the color of their skin but by

the color in their eyes: Poetics

makes stained bedfellows.

Met her by the meadow. Why

not balk? Why not walk

her. *Here we are at loops ends.*

> Strange
> not to think
> to think of
> you.

Enviable miasma. Get this detain out

of default! The where within which

what woos (worrisome weathering).

The clothier makes the person (there's

a change in the sweater, a change

in the smock, from now on

they'll be a change in *you*). *The one man pushed*

the other guy takes away. "You can say it—I

don't have to buy it." Amazingly enough

you can't get a seat on the bus. Whipped

along on a sting as a

pawn. (One could say

she festered under his garrulous

acerbity.) Expansive wastrel. *A fluke*

in Dubuque. WASHINGTON INVADED BY ARMED

FORCE OF MENTAL SPASTICS. Fight

back (flight

bag). Fit

to be fried. *Repudiate*

don't replicate. Spatter

when fingered. *Indelible*

horizon. My country—wronger

and wronger.

> Breathes there a person with soul so dead
> Who never to themself has said
> This is not mine, my native land
> Whose stomach has never within turned
> When home by footstep does return
> From travelling on a foreign strand

It is Shrove Tuesday and Violetta is dying of

consumption. Obviously this didn't work and you

come back to me with a mass of hearsay. In fact,

I'm glad; but on the contrary to skirt for a modification.

But to call anything but—and this is what I take—

wouldn't seem the same for my refusal. All

of this would go double. "As a practical

matter, we can always use forward bases."

> "If words had meaning"
> And people hearts
> If names had faces
> And Desires darts
>
> Then I would build a Conduit
> And call it Quarrelsomeness
> Then I would tell of bats and hats
> Of barnacles and spurs.

Emergence of mush: the hermeneutic ovoid crashes in

on the Pesto Principle; or, he's hooked up

with a poststructuralist woman who's changed

his pew. *Don't speak so loudly, people*

will hear what you think.

Here's the sheets, now

for the towels. (Nothing

so naive as a naive bumper.)

The crunch of

imperative, the blackening of

emblematicism. Go for the

gulp!—a bind is a terrible thing

to pour.

>   My son is
>   going dumb
>   I would pluck
>   out my neighbor's
>   tongue if
>   it would do any
>   good.

Basking in wrappings. *And the dead men*

pull and push but do not heave. Yet

we 'are' each other only insofar as each

can recognize and acknowledge the differences

(as in separately bodied)—to con*fuse* this risks a rule of

power only. For instance, in Manet, the objects

and garb are corporeal while the faces seem

blank: the world thinged in order for any of us

to inhabit it. "People were so happy

when they see Maurice free

they carried him up

on their shoulders & were yelling

& singing." Life as high

as an apple pie. But grieve only

for the survivors, who hoe

in tiers and do not

forsake—hope's stooges.

"And cry, 'Content', to that which grieves

the heart." For there is more to anaesthesia

than simply rendering unconscious

and free of pain. To suppress a twitch

or tone, the anaesthetist

may wish to abolish it

at its origin. A less toxic approach

is to block the signals

or otherwise interfere with their transmission

from source to destination.

On teleologic grounds, one would expect

that more receptors are available

than necessary, and in fact

three-quarters of the receptors must be blocked

before any suppression of twitch response occurs.

The boots are on the run

with no one in 'em. A sky

in an eye, biscuit in other:

pail of crustoid simper. Obligation

concatenates: *Metabolites*

when things go right. Proof

serum. "But they WANT to be invaded." *No*

where to go but r-a-d-i-o. "I've

cried over many a dead dog

since then." Or as my mother

used to say, don't do anything

you wouldn't do on stilts. In the vast space

of the masque, the earthen covers

kneel in patterns of

stencils. All patients gave their informed

consent to participate in this

study and the study protocol

was approved by appropriate

institutional review committees.

She (he) *punched* (pumped) *the* (a) *bloated* (goaded) *dog.*

Brain Side View

Otherwise, what? I mostly here feel, spend

too much time paralyzed, recovering, shaking

hand to clear it out which only fogs

it up: a few alternating beats in the

context of a deproliferating structure that

nonetheless is bouncing by. By way of saucers,

antiseptic engines. Galvanized in the embrace of

overdetermined mood elevators, winsome harbingers

lacerated by needling beneficence. Obtains

what the heart rejects. Nor have I

journeyed far to say this to you: the

rooves and the windows are fortifications

against a life never entered, living next to

air, consuming but implacable to being

consumed. All of which switches, the wince

from the doorlock bridegroom of dejection's

droll succubus. In stanzas of Maalox, intransigent

suede socks. Which consequently broadens its

scope beyond the niceties of the need for,

destined dispossession, marginalized

escape valve. Yet this whole garrulous team sands

down your resistance, as if you wobbled too hurriedly

among four by fives, the pliant rigidity of September

all along falling prey to the remoter restaurants

of implicit decay. A crash course in rubber ducting, chugging

remorselessly with inverted pathos and benighted torpor. Nothing

is learned and nothing is lost, just this rift

in the paving accountable to a firm handshake with a

sun-streaked reconsideration. ... although we promised

less than we delivered, were delivered to. The boat has

landed but the dock has gone to sea. "& the carcasses

of this people shall be food for the fouls

of heaven." So much time, so little

to do. "They're learning and they're not even aware they're

learning." Yanked by. What's this darting this

leafy extravagance? Dominions of tutelage,

opinions of bivalent dirigibles, grown

dark and tender in the crisper, wispier for all

the tempestuousness in a taker's talon.

"But the person must not create the mauled

hour in her books. This is to wish, at all

forces, to consider but one side only of

things. Only transmit to those who read

you the experience that is itself

disgaged from the sadness, and

which is no more the sadness himself." The

great thing about my job is that I

don't have to take it home with me, —if it

didn't keep flashing back in my head. *The New*

Androids: Trends in Psychomimetic Ontology. To shiver

in the summer sunlight, lackadaisically aroused, brusquely

indisposed; but procrastination is the poetry

of our lives. On sleets of inebriate, velour, corona-scented.

Or the hearty hail, minions expelled into the glare of

midday, inspection's ambush. Famished, vanished.

Though I wonder what emotion has you put

that first—the rebuke, as if *that*

goes deepest; but we've been over the ground

of error and care before. You suggest somehow a,

while in that not so, basically, gobbling

up. Sometimes I think you recoil at

certain things not for what they are but

for. Yet it's the road to heaven that is paved

with good intentions. Interior to motion

is always the lash. "Shall we, even after

having understood the calamity, in the end take

refuge in it?" What forces force the hand, by

sleight, unknown to brain? Or you yourself, jumped at,

scootering things out of whack. Aiming at what claims

its loss in dusty drains and carping caulk.

As an extreme instance, the cry

of a pin when I step on a tack, foot

bare, may be the same cry as that on

hearing of the death by fire of my

neighbor's wife. The same phenomenon occurs,

as we have seen before, concurrent upon,

whereas it otherwise might, providing from considering,

a diaper pain in a distance. Total consciousness would be

quite as difficult to detect as shouts for the one

who doesn't hear it. At this point, then, I

would want to renegotiate our arrangement—toward

considerably greater compensation to continue at

the current schedule, or toward a more freelance

arrangement with a more restricted area of

responsibility. At first plush, thumps up. I may

tell you we are really all homely girls. That the ticket

we can never really envision is the one that

has already gotten us in, so now we move noiselessly

in white person file. All the same, bent

out of shape, sweating blood. Prudes and

prisms, cork-brained, buoyant souls on blink. All

talk and no cipher (spider). Then take your frost

off my neck and play a pillar with your ail.

Beside the cushion is your natural home, "and

mine with my heart in it". This is the turkey on our

back (not your—): envy, greed—God's acre. With

coals and smote to grease my hands, a haven

like a writing desk, towelled in disbelief.

The barbell of denuded calumny

retires in proponderousness' wedges.

The Harbor of Illusion

At midnight's scrawl, the fog has
lost its bone and puffs of
pall are loamed at
tidal edge. No more to count
than density arrows its
petulance at crevice laced
with dock, not hour's
solstice nor brimmed detour—
over the haunch of lock and
tress the vein pours sweetly
and Devil's door knows no
more than pester and undone—
the seering moors where I
refrain of lot and camphor,
Only this, a ripple
against a blind of shore that sands
us smooth and mistless: let
he who has not stunned make
sound, cacophany of
nearing, having fell, of
pouring, having stalled. Though
free to bore and load, let
rail retail conclusion, finicky jejubes
at waste of moor, or lord these
tower, tour the template, thoroughfare
of noon's atoll.

Acknowledgements

Douglas Messerli's Sun & Moon Press first published this book in 1987. It was an honor to be part of that company.

Portions of this book originally appeared in *The Difficulties, boundary 2, Sulfur, Roof, Hills, Acts, Reality Studios, Splash, L.A. Weekly, The World, Temblor, Benzene, Rampike, Wch Way/New Wilderness, Paper Air, Washington Review of the Arts, 1733 South 5th West, Brooklyn Review, Boxcar, Text, Writing, Qu, African Golfer, Privates, Sapiens, Abacus, Aphros, Knock Knock, Clothes, Flute, The Poetry Project Newsletter, O.Ars, Multiples, Ironwood, Tramen, Tyuonyi, Post Neo, Southern Humanities Review*, and *Mandorla*.

Thanks to Tom Beckett, William Spanos, Clayton Eshleman, James Sherry, Bob Perelman, David Levi-Strauss, Ken Edwards, Wystan Curnow & Tony Green & Roger Horrocks & Judi Stout, Cliff Fyman, Leland Hickman, Alan Bealey, Karl Jirgens, Jerome Rothenberg & Don Byrd & Jed Rasula, Gil Ott, Douglas Messerli, Paul Piper & Bill Borneman, Robert Thompson, Mark Karlins, Colin Browne, Carla Harryman, Dale Heiniger, Edward Kaplan, Peter Ganick, Neil Keating, Vicki Hudspith & Madeleine Keller, Allen Fisher, Brian McInerney, Ted Greenwald, Don Wellman, Ron Silliman, Jim Hartz, Phillip Foss, Pete Spence, Dan Latimer, and Roberto Tejada. And thanks too to Susan Bee for her help at every phase of the production.

"The Only Utopia Is in a Now" is a response, in part, to "Homage to Jonathan Swift: another story told about the language of the past" in *Utopia* by Bernadette Mayer (New York: United Artists, 1984) and originally appeared in that book.

"Rose the Click for 23" is a homophonic translation of *Rose-Declic* by Dominique Fourcade (Le Revest-les-Eaux, France: Spectres Familiers, 1984), 4:XXIII.